Soft Life

Soft Life

10 STEPS TO A GENTLE, ABUNDANT AND EASEFUL LIFE

Toni Tone

ILLUSTRATIONS BY AMBERLEE GREEN OF LINE & HONEY

BLOOMSBURY TONIC
LONDON • OXFORD • NEW YORK • NEW DELHI • SYDNEY

BLOOMSBURY TONIC
Bloomsbury Publishing Plc
50 Bedford Square, London, WC1B 3DP, UK
Bloomsbury Publishing Ireland Limited,
29 Earlsfort Terrace, Dublin 2, D02 AY28, Ireland

First published in Great Britain 2026

A catalogue record for this book is available from the British Library

ISBN: HB: 978-1-5266-9388-4; eBook: 978-1-5266-9387-7

2 4 6 8 10 9 7 5 3 1

Typeset by Christopher O'Leary
Printed and bound in Great Britain by Clays Ltd, Elcograf S.p.A

FSC www.fsc.org
MIX
Paper | Supporting responsible forestry
FSC® C018072

To find out more about our authors and books, visit www.bloomsbury.com and sign up for our newsletters
For product-safety-related questions, contact productsafety@bloomsbury.com

This book is for every woman who is ready to reset.
For every woman who longs for more ease, abundance, and a gentler way of living. For every woman who wants to release the pressure to do it all and embrace a life that feels lighter, softer, and more aligned. Soft living is not unattainable; it starts with this book and a willingness to shift your perspective. Make the decision to choose peace over pressure and ease over endless striving. Make the decision to choose yourself...

Contents

Introduction 9

Soft Story: Hard Beginnings 15

Soft Esteem: It Starts with Self-Love 27

Soft Friendship: Nurture Friendships That Nourish You 43

Soft Wealth: Spending with Intention is Self-Care 67

Soft Boundaries: You Are Not Here to Please Everyone 85

Soft Love: Choose A Love That Nurtures You 107

Soft Health: Honour What Your Body Tells You 127

Soft Work: Why Work Needs to Align with What You Value 147

Soft Courage: Protect Your Peace in a Hard World 161

Soft Future: Embrace Change During Times of Uncertainty 177

Epilogue: Stepping into Your Soft Life 195

Acknowledgements 200

Introduction

What is soft life to you?
Is it living a life of opulence and material luxury?
Constant jet setting?
Financial freedom?

What are the central tenets that you think make up a soft life?

I ask you this because 'soft life' has become a phenomenon – particularly online. It has evolved in online spaces to represent all the above (with some spa days thrown in). But the truth is, soft living has been misunderstood. Somewhere along the way, we reduced it to a highlight reel, and in doing so, we lost the heart of what it truly means to live a soft life. We're getting soft living all wrong...

In case you're new here, let me briefly introduce myself before I continue. My name is Toni Tone, and I'm a 36-year-old author, podcaster, speaker, content creator and soft life advocate. I've achieved many things in my life that I'm proud of, and I feel very fulfilled by the life I live, but to get to this point I had to learn how to live softly, and that took time.

I also don't come from particularly soft beginnings. From the outside looking in, many people wrongly assume that my life has always been 'easy'. But the truth is, I have worked hard at cultivating a life that doesn't simply appear soft, but also feels gentle. My experience has taught me that the version of soft life we're sold online is pretty, but arguably shallow and lacking context. A truly soft life isn't something people simply attain with wealth – it's something they must practise, even when they may not be financially wealthy.

To elaborate, living a truly soft life isn't about monetary abundance or living to impress other people. It's about putting you first – looking after your mental and physical health, limiting stress, feeding into positive relationships and leading a life that allows you to show up as the happiest and most authentic version of yourself.

My aim is to offer you ten key lessons for adopting the tenets of soft life, including harnessing your community, looking after your health, self-acceptance, understanding money, loving freely, prioritising rest, and most importantly, being true to who you are.

> Soft living is an antidote to the hustle culture and obsession with 'rising and grinding', and this book will teach you how to centre rest and renewal – with a focus on what truly makes you happy.

The world often teaches us to push ourselves, prove ourselves to others and achieve excellence in the process – but at some point, enough is enough. The burden of living to satisfy other people's opinion of us can feel very heavy, if not exhausting...

My life taught me that my dreams could still be realised if I prioritised rest, recovery and relationships. As I entered my thirties, I began embodying what I believe it means to truly live softly, and things started to change for me. I started listening to my body instead of pushing it, I began saying say 'no' to people without guilt, and I stopped searching for acceptance and validation. Somewhere along the way, I began to prioritise how my life felt rather than how it looked to other people, and by my mid-thirties I'd stepped into a new era that was no longer defined by constant achievement but by personal fulfilment.

I learned that living a truly soft life is rooted in intention. It's about choosing good health over burnout. It's about surrounding yourself with community, not just company. It's creating space for self-love, not self-sacrifice. It's setting boundaries because your peace matters, it's about choosing a career that aligns with your values rather than one that drains your identity, and it's about prioritising healthy romantic relationships where you feel seen, supported and safe. When you choose to live softly, you honour your rest, listen to your intuition and give yourself permission to live in a way that doesn't constantly stretch you to the limit.

As you read this book, I want you to challenge the way you may have perceived soft living. I want you to unlearn the belief that mental and emotional ease is only reserved for the few, or that it must be earned. This book hasn't been written to teach you how to create a 'picture-perfect' life or escape reality. I wrote it to help you create a fulfilling life and reshape how you choose to exist in this world. We'll explore what that looks like in practice, and we'll also confront the truth that for many, especially women and people of colour, the world is not built to be soft, yet we can still create softness within it.

This book is your invitation to live intentionally, to slow down, feel deeply and create a life that works for you – not one that looks good to everyone else. My hope is that by the end of this book, you will open a door to a gentler and more intentional way of being. One where you feel like you're in control of your life, and you are not just surviving but thriving in a state of gentleness, abundance and ease.

Soft Story: Hard Beginnings

At the time of writing this book, I am living the softest season of my life. There is nothing that I feel I need which I do not have – and I have most things I want – while the few things I want which I do not have, don't feel out of reach.

Currently, I'm writing this book from the apartment my husband and I share. I feel relaxed. I'm sitting at our dining table, and the sunlight is spilling through the window on my left – after hitting the surface of the large man-made pond next to our building. Each ripple of water bends the light, scattering it upward onto the ceiling in soft, dancing patterns. Jazz is playing in the background – 'Iris' Secret' by loopgarden – and next to me is a mug of Three Mint tea, because caffeine makes me jittery. I love my life. I'm not a millionaire, nor am I a 'perfect' person. I simply love the mindset I have developed, the people I am surrounded by, the environment I am living in, the career I have, the way I feel about myself and the impact I have on the lives of others.

That said, my life hasn't always felt this gentle, and I want to give you a whistle-stop tour of some of the hard, before we get into the soft.

I grew up in a family of five – my parents, one brother and one sister. I was born in 1989, in West Africa (Nigeria, to be exact), and moved to the UK (Oxford) as a child. That transition was relatively challenging for me. Despite being quite young, the change in temperature, environment, economic stability, familiarity and going from being one of many Black students in an all-Black school to being one of few Black students in a predominantly white school, was a shock to the system. People often assume that moving from

Africa to Europe automatically guarantees an immediately improved life, but that isn't necessarily true. Before my family and I left Nigeria, we were living comfortably. We had a car, a fully furnished home in Ibadan with a big front and back garden where my brother and I played for hours. On the surface, nothing about our life looked like 'struggle', so the idea that the UK would somehow be an upgrade wasn't so straightforward. When my parents came to the UK, they arrived with nothing but one suitcase each and an audacious belief that they could rebuild an entire life from scratch. Starting over as a couple is brave enough, but doing it in a country completely unlike the one you've always known, while raising two young children at the time, takes a different kind of courage. What hits me now is that my parents were actually younger than I am today when they made that leap. It's inspiring, but if I'm totally honest, it's also overwhelming to think about.

Despite their audacious beliefs, our transition to British life wasn't smooth in the slightest. My Mum was already in the UK having spent a year completing a university scholarship, so my Dad, brother and I travelled to meet her there. When we arrived, my entire family initially stayed in a single room in an Oxford bed and breakfast. It was a tight space and a far cry from what I was used to. Eventually the government put us in council accommodation (government housing). We weren't living in the best area, but as a child I didn't know this. I was just happy that we were finally in a place we didn't have to share with strangers. However, the move to the UK continued to take a toll on our family dynamic. It took a little while for my parents to find full-time work, and after some time doing odd jobs here and there, my father eventually found a position, the only problem being he was met with relentless racism at the hands of his colleagues. Even when he spoke up and tried to advocate for himself, he wasn't taken seriously, and the experience chipped away at him. That kind of workplace trauma doesn't stay at work – it seeped into our home. He became easily irritated, short-tempered and more distant. When my sister (who is almost seven years younger than me) was born, the pressure intensified. My mum wasn't working at the time and was burdened by the fact she couldn't contribute financially. We were depending entirely on my dad, and his income was barely enough to keep us afloat. In hindsight, we struggled. My brother and I laugh about it now, but there was a time when our diet consisted of instant noodles, canned meatballs, and anything with those blue-striped Tesco Value labels. For anyone unfamiliar, Tesco Value was the supermarket's bargain range that launched during the early nineties' recession. You could buy basics like beans or bread for as little as 10p. Back then, that brand practically kept our household running.

During that period of my childhood, my parents frequently argued, and my siblings and I weren't always shielded from those arguments. I'm thankful that the relationship between my parents has evolved over time for the better, and for the most part, I have plenty of happy childhood memories – but I also grapple with a few not so pleasant ones. I show my parents grace though, because as the adult I am today, I understand that they were trying their best as a struggling couple in their thirties with three children. That said, as a child, it's very hard to wrap your head around adult conflict – and it's very easy for that anxiety to impact you (I'll go into this more later). Let's just say, I have a soft life as a thirty-something-year-old woman, but I'd be pretending if I said my childhood was always soft. Some days it was, and on other days it felt hard.

On top of everything happening at home, I went through waves of bullying in primary and middle school. In primary school, it came from a girl in my year group, and in middle school, it was two brothers who seemed determined to make my life miserable. When I look back now, two people were instrumental in preventing my confidence from crumbling completely – my mum, with her constant stream of affirmations, and my middle-school deputy head teacher, Mr Brown. Mr Brown and I never sat down for some big, emotional conversation about what I was going through, but I believe he knew. And in his own quiet way, he protected me. He'd involve me in organising assemblies, encourage me to speak up during them, and let me spend breaks in his office – small acts that felt like shelter. Those moments gave me room to breathe and space to see strengths in myself that the bullying almost buried.

While I was busy growing into a teenager, my mum was in the background quietly hustling her way into a new life. She got a job, then left for a better one, then earned a promotion. Bit by bit, she rebuilt everything. By my mid-teens, we had moved into our first home that wasn't council housing. It was a place we owned, and she was the one who bought it. I remember feeling ecstatic, but more than anything, I was proud. Deeply proud. In her, I saw a woman who refused to give up. A woman who stayed hopeful even when hope didn't come easily. Someone with a vision for the kind of life she wanted, who adapted through every curveball, believed in herself, and worked tirelessly to turn her dreams into something real – not just for her, but for her family. Through her, I learned that almost anything is possible, and somehow, even with all the pressure she carried, she maintained a joyful temperament through it all.

During this time, my dad started his first UK business – an internet café in Oxford, which was an escape from his previous employment. My dad was very passionate about his business, and proud of it too – but the challenges of him being a business owner fell onto the entire family, including my brother, sister and me. My brother and I were regularly made to work in the internet café after school, although my brother got the worst of it – often being the one who was selected to stay until closing. The thing is, the internet café didn't shut at 5 p.m., or even 6 p.m. – it was open until 9 p.m. Imagine, waking up at 7.30 a.m. to get ready for school, starting school at 8.45 a.m., remaining at school until 3.15 p.m., and then working from 4 p.m. to 9 p.m. – all while being 14–16 years of age. Even my little sister was encouraged to pull her weight for the sake of the family business. Around this same period, our family was hit with one of the most terrifying chapters of our lives. My younger sister fell sick – sudden, unpredictable episodes that no doctor could fully explain. At the height of it, when I was about sixteen, she had to be admitted to hospital. I'll never forget the look on the nurses' faces during the worst episodes. It was a mix of urgency and fear. I remember sitting beside my sister's hospital bed as a teenager, completely helpless, whispering prayers and bargaining with God. I begged for her healing, and on the worst nights, I even asked God to take me instead. Fast-forward a few years, and thankfully my sister recovered from these episodes and was in good health. Doctors suggested that her illness was the result of rapid growth spurts. At the time, the explanation felt like a bit of a cop-out, but I didn't care. My sister was alive and healthy, and having my family was all that mattered to me.

As I write all this, my eyes are welling up. Partly because, wow –

I've been through some challenges that for the most part, people don't really know much about. I'm also welling up because my relationship with my siblings was a saving grace for me in so many ways. There are only two people in this world who know what my childhood was truly like, and that's my brother and my sister.

Speaking of my siblings, I am the eldest of the three of us. Which brought its own challenges – hardcore eldest child syndrome. For much of my life, I have felt responsible for the wellbeing of my siblings. I also felt like failure wasn't an option and I prized being the sibling who did well in school, and who always held it together. But the truth is, I was pushed to find worth in these things because I didn't have the privilege of being the sibling who fell apart. In fact, for much of my life I've identified as the 'strong one' – the strong friend, the strong daughter, the strong sibling, the strong partner... And when you're continuously performing resilience and showcasing dependability, people often assume you're stress-free because you appear functional. And that assumed functionality leads to people rarely checking in or offering support.

This summed up a lot of my life. I was seen as dependable, so I was rarely offered help, which led me to assume I wouldn't receive it if I asked for it. I learned to suppress my feelings and needs so I could be of service to others. But the thing is, this suppression helped other people but it never helped me: it only hurt me. There were points in my life with friends, family and partners, where I felt like I was constantly extending myself and giving while rarely receiving. I began to feel very resentful – not just towards other people but also towards myself. I resented my inability to advocate for myself like I wanted, I resented the fact that in constantly being of service, I enabled certain behaviours in others, and I hated that in suppressing how I truly felt, emotional numbness became my baseline – I believed I rarely felt, when in fact I did feel, but I spent so long ignoring it, I didn't know how to process things healthily.

If I'm completely honest, I've had more than one meltdown in my life due to suppressing my emotions and then eventually exploding. Those meltdowns exposed several things that I will touch on later in this book – among them, the fact that I often internalised my stress, I frequently over-extended myself, and I needed to do a better job at asserting boundaries.

At age eighteen, I entered university. I managed to get a place at Brunel University in Uxbridge (a town on the western outskirts of London). For the most part, I really enjoyed my time at university. It was my first real taste of independence – living away from my parents, managing my own time, and figuring out who I was outside the structure of home. The diversity was also refreshing. As you can imagine, going from school in Oxford to suddenly being dropped into the multiculturalism of London exposed me to a completely different world. It excited me and forced me to grow in ways I didn't even realise I needed. However, university was also the place where I experienced my first heartbreak. My university boyfriend was hands down the most toxic of any of my past relationships. If you've ever read *No F*cks Given* – my zero-accountability guide to getting over a boy – you already know how bad it was. I was cheated on, emotionally toyed with, and dealt with domestic violence. That relationship made me question my value, my reality and even my safety, and I cried much more than I should have while at university. Thankfully, that relationship didn't hinder my studies too much, and I managed to graduate with a 2:1 (the equivalent of a B).

Despite doing well, I struggled to secure a job after university and eventually spent a few years working in retail. From there I went on to do a range of other jobs I wasn't particularly passionate about (you'll find out more about those later). Long story short, for many years I worked in jobs that didn't fulfil me, and I racked up debt along the way. To be honest, for most of my twenties I had no clue what I was doing with my life. I was kind of just existing – surviving but not thriving. Living pay cheque to pay cheque, wondering if I'd ever be out of debt. During this time, I fell in love again – and spent almost six years in an on-and-off relationship that had me questioning my value. The end of that relationship was my biggest heartbreak, but it was also a defining moment for me. For the first time I asked myself what the heck I was doing, and why. That's the thing about grief (in any form). As painful as it is, it can also shake us up in a way that acts as a reminder to embrace life – which is exactly what I did in the years following.

I reconsidered what it really meant to love myself and how my self-perception was impacting my life. I began to shed the weight of other people's opinions, which led to me writing more and eventually penning a book. I left my full-time job and started my own company to create a career I found fulfilling. I poured myself into the friendships I valued and the people who had been there for me through everything. I re-evaluated what I wanted from a romantic partner, and what it meant to be truly loved. I reassessed my relationship with money – examining how my past attitudes had contributed to my debt. Put simply, it took economic struggles, being bullied/disliked, heartbreak, a lack of self-love and much more for me to realise that my life wasn't working for me. Things had to fall apart so I could put them back together – better. I was forced to rebuild, and the rebuilding process opened my eyes.

The parts of my life that transformed from hard to soft are exactly what I'm going to walk you through in this book. When I decided to write *Soft Life*, I knew I didn't want to speak from theory or surface-level observation. I wanted to speak from lived experience. So, I'm going to cover money, relationships, career, self-esteem, people-pleasing, friendships and more – all the areas of my life that I previously struggled with and improved.

I share some of the hard pieces of my story with you because I want you to see what's possible. I want you to know that change isn't simply reserved for the lucky or exceptional. I'm living proof that your life can soften, expand and shift in ways you may not even imagine yet, because a soft life isn't the product of a soft past – it's the outcome of reflection, intentional action and a mindset that refuses to settle for survival when you were meant for abundance.

Fast-forward to today.

I am so proud of the woman I have become. The young girl who was thrust into a childhood she had little to no control over, has grown into a woman who unapologetically controls the things within her command. Now I understand that as an adult, I have influence over my life and my outcomes. The young girl who was bullied has become someone who advocates for herself, who stays true to herself, and who has no issue with people disliking her as an adult. The young adult who was in relationships that didn't serve her, has ended up with her dream man and has a love that is soft, steady, and grounding – yet still passionate. The child who didn't grow up wealthy and who racked up debt in her twenties, rarely worries about money in her thirties. The girl who once desired validation, no longer strives for applause, but works to pour into others in a way that genuinely shifts their world. The girl who had no idea what she wanted to do with her life, now has a fulfilling career that brings her joy and excitement.

This is my story, now let's get into how you can change yours.

Soft Esteem: It Starts with Self-Love

Before I take you through the journey of attaining ease, abundance and gentleness, we must consider the foundation of all of it – which is you. Your self-perception is integral to how softness manifests in your life. Why? Because how you view yourself, how you treat yourself and how you speak to yourself sets the tone for almost everything you experience.

Many people want to cultivate an external image of a soft life that aligns with Hollywood fantasies and luxe lifestyles portrayed in magazines by the rich and famous, or what they see on social media – but these images mean very little if at your core, your self-image is rooted in shame, insecurity, comparison or self-critique.

How Do You See Yourself?

This question is a vulnerable one, which many people struggle to answer. I for one would have struggled to answer it at several points in my life, out of difficulty with speaking about myself honestly and confidently. I am presenting this question to you for a similar reason. Sadly, many people don't view themselves positively. Or at least, they struggle to articulate how they view themselves without being self-deprecating. And on the off chance they consider speaking about themselves with pride, or simply just kindness, they hesitate. They question whether they're being boastful, *too* proud, or conceited in some way. Funny, that. Why is that many of us struggle to talk about ourselves with pleasure and delight? Why is it that this question makes people (particularly women), feel so awkward?

How do you see yourself? I want you to look inward and acknowledge the parts of yourself you're proud of, as well as the parts you try to avoid. I'm asking you to define yourself, by yourself, and not according to the opinions of others. While answering this question, don't consider how other people view you. Be really upfront and honest – how do you see you?

How you see yourself dictates your choices, and every step of the way, living softly is determined by what you choose. In fact, one hard pill to swallow is that your outcomes in life are largely the culmination of all your choices. What you pursue, what you allow, what you reject, what you do and what you choose to believe places you on a variety of paths. A soft and fulfilling life isn't something you simply stumble on – it's something you create, and that starts with how you view yourself.

> When you see yourself as someone who is deserving of respect, care and love, then you view receiving this as the bare minimum and you're unwilling to tolerate anything less.

For a long period of my life, I didn't consider how I saw myself. I didn't think I hated myself, but I didn't question whether I loved myself either. I didn't think about myself much at all – and that was the problem. I wasn't at the centre of my own life. I wasn't a priority.

When you don't assess how you view yourself, you will struggle to direct your life. Your values, boundaries, strengths, wants, needs, character and non-negotiables won't be at the forefront of your considerations or decisions. You will end up making choices based on fleeting feelings or other people's expectations and opinions, instead of what you truly want, need and deserve. How you view yourself and understanding who you are, is a fundamental part of building your dream life, because one thing that separates people who do it successfully versus people who don't, is feeling deserving.

This may seem harsh, but you will struggle to build a soft life if, deep down, you don't believe you deserve it.

Believing that you are deserving and worthy of a good life, means that in turn, you will treat yourself with respect, care and love – and that is also what you expect from others. In treating yourself well, you centre your wellbeing. You make decisions that you believe are in your best interest, and you set boundaries as a way of honouring yourself and your beliefs. In treating yourself well, you show yourself compassion, and you give yourself grace to learn from your mistakes, rather than hate yourself for them.

The Illusion of the 'Soft Aesthetic'

When we scroll through social media, it's easy to run into images and videos tagged 'soft life', that showcase opulent environments, pricey luxuries and aesthetic moments. And while there's nothing wrong with comfort, opulence or beauty, we mustn't mistake appearing 'soft' for genuine softness. Many of us (myself included) have once mistaken material comfort and curated moments for soft living – but that's often the surface level version, not the real thing. The simple truth is that you can be surrounded by beauty while still showing yourself unkindness, you can be experiencing luxuries yet still be internally stressed, and you can possess a lifestyle that people envy from the outside looking in, while feeling insecure, unsatisfied or generally unhappy. People often spend years chasing the version of a soft life that might appear amazing, not realising that it is actually far from living softly internally. And frankly, it's easy to fake the external, but you can't run away from the reality of your feelings. Building a life that *appears* soft doesn't require much beyond money – but a truly soft existence requires courage, introspection, honesty, vulnerability, healing, self-compassion, boundaries, vision and so much more. The real moment of change for you will occur when you put your feelings at the centre, and you create a life that flourishes from the inside out. A life that verifies that you love yourself, and you view yourself positively.

Cultivating Self-love

So, assuming you've answered the question 'how do you see yourself?' negatively, I need to take you through ways you can begin to cultivate self-love.

Boundary setting

One major part of showing yourself real love is boundary setting. When you set boundaries, you are reminding yourself and those around you of what you will and won't accept. And while it may seem easy in theory, plenty of people struggle with setting boundaries for a variety of reasons...

From my brief life story, it should be clear to you that boundary setting is something I struggled with. I think my experience with moving to a new country so young, and being bullied as a child, made me desperate to be liked and to 'fit in'. Women are generally taught to be agreeable, non-confrontational or 'people pleasers' anyway, but growing up as a girl who sometimes felt out of place, made my boundary setting even more shaky. In addition, growing up as the eldest child meant that in my family, I was the 'fixer'. When there was an issue, I was expected to provide emotional, practical and sometimes even financial support. And if I'm being honest, at times I didn't want to be of help, but rather than express that, I picked up the weight of that responsibility. Put simply, I didn't want to let anyone down – the habit of a people pleaser. This was reinforced by the fact that much of the praise I received when I was young, stemmed from my behaviour and performance. I received words of affirmation when I was responsible, helpful to others and high achieving in school, so I guess I linked a lot of my self-worth to what I was doing instead of who I was as a person.

When your sense of self revolves around being a 'fixer' – dependable, helpful and supportive – it's very easy to forget your own needs, wants and limits. It's very easy for you to not assert boundaries, but the only way for you to prevent losing touch with who you are, is by actually allowing yourself to express those same needs, wants and limits.

Setting boundaries teaches everyone around you what you're willing to accept, and it starts with being in tune with how you feel, and honest with yourself about feeling it.

When I was emotionally drained, stressed, frustrated, angry, or felt like I was being undervalued (by partners, friends or family), I rarely spoke up. I often suppressed those feelings, when in fact I should have acknowledged and expressed them.

What I know now that I didn't know then, is that boundary setting requires honesty and clarity. You will struggle to set boundaries if you're unable to recognise your emotions and know your limits – another reason, why earlier on in this chapter, I asked you how you see yourself. Sadly, many people don't slow down long enough to reflect and ask themselves what they're willing and unwilling to put up with. They operate in a reactive state, and not a proactive state – rarely being honest with themselves about their feelings. In completely accepting that certain feelings exist within you, you begin to express them without guilt, and act. This may be through limiting someone's access to you, giving yourself permission to put yourself first, or even declining requests for support. And if you struggle with self-advocating, you don't need to start big. Small moments of self-prioritisation, like simply saying 'no' to a request you often say yes to, can be a helpful reminder that the world won't end, and people's lives won't immediately collapse if you put yourself first for once.

Talk to yourself kindly

When I asked you how you see yourself, did you internally express your self-perception kindly or unkindly? If you were unkind to yourself, I want you to know that self-criticism isn't something people express for no reason. It's often birthed from past experience – including being critiqued or judged by others, being abandoned or neglected, or being raised in environments where affirmations and praise weren't freely given. For some people, it's also a product of a past mistake – connected to existing shame, regret or self-blame.

Let's pause for a moment.

Why do you think you speak to yourself with unkindness? What made you feel like you aren't good enough? *Who* made you feel like you aren't good enough? Are you blaming yourself for something?

Frustratingly, self-criticism is often met with more self-criticism. When we catch ourselves being unkind to ourselves, it's not uncommon for us to beat ourselves up over it. Many people are self-critical about being self-critical, but not in a way that encourages them to be gentler with themselves. Instead, they view the negative self-talk as a personal flaw, instead of what I believe it typically is – a defence mechanism. 'If I'm unkind to myself first, people won't be unkind to me, or it'll hurt a little less.' Negative self-talk is one way we maintain a sense of control in a world that can feel quite harsh.

However, the thing is, unkind self-talk feels small and harmless in the moment, but over time it impacts mental health. One longitudinal 2025 study titled 'Exploring the longitudinal dynamics of self-criticism, self-compassion, psychological flexibility, and mental health in a three-wave study', followed 839 adults and measured their self-criticism, coping strategies and mental health outcomes. The study by Ming Yu Claudia Wong, Hong Wang Fung and colleagues, found that people with higher self-criticism generally had worse mental health outcomes over time – supporting the idea that self-criticism is more than just a harmless habit, as it acts like a chronic stressor, putting mental wellbeing at risk.

> Negative self-talk can also alter how you view yourself. When you repeatedly tell yourself you're not good enough, you're not deserving or you're incapable, your brain will eventually begin to believe it as truth.

Aaron Temkin Beck is widely known as the creator of cognitive therapy, which has evolved into what we recognise today as cognitive behavioural therapy (CBT) – one of the most applied psychological treatments in the world. According to the Beck

Institute for Cognitive Behavior Therapy, through clinical research and observations, Beck noticed that many people with depression suffered not because of hidden unconscious conflicts, but because of continuous negative thoughts and beliefs. This led to a change in how Beck operated – examining patients' thought patterns, then working collaboratively to challenge and eventually change them. Beck named his new approach 'cognitive therapy', which was shown in research to be effective for treating depression. At the core of CBT is the understanding that our internal thoughts and beliefs are powerful – shaping not just our moods but also our self-perception and our life outcomes.

CBT teaches us that our thoughts act as instructions, and they are so much more than mere internal commentary. Developing a critical and unkind inner voice can distort how you see yourself and the world around you – as well as increase depression. Being kind to yourself isn't about forcing happiness or pretending everything is OK when it isn't – it's about showing yourself compassion, even when you're unhappy or things feel like they're falling apart. Perhaps you are unkind to yourself because you made a mistake? You're human, and as humans, mistakes happen. We are also capable of changing for the better, and we are deserving of self-compassion while we learn to do better. Seeing yourself as someone who must be punished or constantly corrected won't change the past; it just encourages you to resent the person you are, and that kind of resentment doesn't encourage self-improvement. Instead, accept the fact you, like everyone else, are imperfect, and you are constantly learning. And that doesn't mean you excuse your mistakes. Every mistake is a learning moment, but it's important that you free yourself from defining yourself according to your worst moments or decisions, because you are so much more than that. Do what CBT teaches us... Cultivate a gentle internal voice, because it's one of the most powerful ways for you to improve your wellbeing and life in general.

Allow yourself to rest

I've always been big on rest. In fact, resting is one thing I do well – sometimes a little too well. Even when I didn't necessarily do a good job at carving out boundaries when it came to assisting other people, I still managed to make time for myself to simply exist. Why? If I'm honest, it wasn't due to possessing some enlightened understanding of the importance of rest... It's just that I can't function well when I'm constantly on the go. Could you call me lazy? The word 'lazy' doesn't feel accurate. A better description is to say that my mind and body shut down when I'm drained, so I've always needed pockets of stillness to feel like myself again. I'm also more of an introvert than an extrovert. To be ultra-precise, I'm technically an ambivert (a person who has a balance of extrovert and introvert features in their personality), but I'm slightly more of an introvert according to my social tendencies and the many personality tests I've taken throughout my life.

According to Chris Yam, author of *The Introvert's Light to Networking Success*, one thing that separates introverts and extroverts is how social situations impact them. According to Yam, extroverts are typically left energised by interaction and external stimulation, while introverts are left depleted – and the latter is certainly me. I can put on the façade of an extroverted person at a social gathering, but the moment I'm in my own space, I feel de-energised, as if I need to recharge my entire mind and body. In other words, I make rest a priority because people drain me. Without time to myself, I feel overwhelmed and exhausted, so I am naturally pulled towards rest. I can't say the same is true for everyone though, and I personally know many people who struggle with resting.

Without calling individuals out, one thing that ties many of the people I'm thinking about is how they perceive their career. For many people who treat their job as their ultimate priority (even above family), rest is often under-prioritised. You may be assuming that they all have very special, intense jobs, but for the most part, that isn't the case. It's just that so much of their identity is tied not to who they are, but to what they do. Have you ever met anyone like this before? They're the type of people who will meet you for the first time and ask 'so what do you do?' before they ask you anything else about your life. They're the type of people to lead with their profession in every interaction. Their sense of self-worth is tied to their achievements or job title, so resting feels unproductive to them because it challenges the identity they've built around their job or being high-performing. Or maybe they're simply addicted to the external validation that comes with always doing something.

These people are the type to boast in the workplace about never taking a day off work – as if being unwell and resting is something to be ashamed about. The rise of 'hustle culture' and society teaching us that rest is indulgent or even lazy has encouraged this attitude. It's easy to fall into the trap of performing and pushing to prove our value to others. I also know a few people who aren't necessarily career focused or validation orientated, but who still don't make time for rest. In many communities these are the aunties, grandmas or maybe even friends who are always tinkering, always helping, always assisting – when they should be putting their feet up (or even enjoying their retirement).

Sadly, I believe that many people who fall into this category simply don't know *how* to rest. A few people in my life are like this. They grew up in chaotic environments, so peace is unfamiliar to them. They're so used to running on adrenaline that anything different, like rest, feels uncomfortable. So much so that when you encourage them to take a break, you can see the discomfort in their body language via the fidgeting, darting of the eyes, or huffing and puffing. Rest doesn't come natural to everyone... There are also people who believe rest must always be earned. As if they're not deserving of simply relaxing for the sake of it.

The thing is, all that over-functioning can easily evolve into exhaustion – not just internally but also physically. Author Alex Soojung-Kim Pang is a four-day working week evangelist and the writer of *Rest: Why You Get More Done When You Work Less*. Pang argues that many people view rest negatively, as if it is the opposite of work, when in fact it's a key part of high performance, creativity and long-term productivity. According to Pang, rest in the form of breaks, hobbies, leisure time, working out, going on a walk, or even taking a nap, helps to restore attention, improves memory, enhances insight, and ultimately prevents burnout. Pang even goes as far as stating that many of history's most accomplished figures, from Bill Gates to Charles Darwin, didn't work tirelessly, but instead, structured their days around intentional work and deliberate rest.

Rest is essential for recharging your body – physically, emotionally and mentally. Speaking for myself, when I'm burnt out, I experience frequent headaches, insomnia, irritability, low mood, aches and pains, and fatigue. Living softly requires gentleness with not just others but also yourself.

> Resting is another form of self-love because through resting, you are listening to your body, paying attention to your energy and honouring your limits. Giving yourself permission to rest is one way of affirming that your wellbeing is more important than appearing successful or pleasing others. Allow yourself to slow down and remind yourself that you deserve ease, not just endurance.

My Nigerian American husband frequently shares one-liners – and one of his favourites is 'body no be stone'. This is a West African Pidgin English expression that basically means 'your body isn't a machine'. Actually, I take that back. It isn't simply an expression. It's wisdom with a sprinkle of West African humour. It's a necessary reminder that it's natural for us to feel pain, feel tired and require rest. It's a line used to remind people that we all have a limit. So, whenever you find yourself slipping back into old habits of overworking, overextending, or ignoring your needs, remember this West African proverb that so many of us grew up hearing... Body no be stone.

Closing Thoughts

Self-love isn't a finish line; it's a daily journey of honouring your needs, choosing what is best for you and protecting your peace. As you learn to speak to yourself with more kindness, I want you to set boundaries without guilt, I want you to speak to yourself with the care you express to others, and I want you to know that rest isn't something you must earn. At the core of living softly is loving yourself in a way that acknowledges you are worthy of care from everyone – including yourself.

Self-reflection prompts

How would you describe yourself to someone who has never met you, and what does that reveal about how you see yourself?

When was the last time you noticed you spoke to yourself unkindly, and what triggered it?

When was the last time you treated yourself with kindness?

What boundaries do you need to set, to protect your peace?

What habits or environments make you feel most like your true self, and how can you bring more of that into your life?

What past version of you are you grateful for, and what did they survive so you could be here now?

Where does your self-worth currently come from, and is that foundation steady or rocky?

Is there anything you wish you would stop tolerating?

Soft Friendship: Nurture Friendships That Nourish You

Soft living begins with the people around you. No matter how much you possess, or how frequently you rest or self-reflect, your softness can only flourish in environments that feel secure, and nothing shapes our sense of security more than the company we keep.

You simply can't live softly in hard company, and you can't live a life filled with happiness and peace if you're surrounded by people who are committed to draining your joy. Your relationships matter, and softness flourishes in community – not in solitude.

When we consider 'dream relationships', we often place emphasis on romantic love, and I admit that I've been guilty of this. I've written more books about romantic relationships than I have about anything else, because romantic love is captivating, intriguing and often discussed. However, as meaningful as romantic love can be, we mustn't underestimate the power of our wider community – because the company we keep outside of romantic partners has a profound impact on our wellbeing.

> Creating a soft life isn't just about what you do – it's also about who you decide to do it with.

Friendships in particular play a powerful role because unlike the family you're born into, friends are chosen, and that choice is largely built on shared values, mutual interests and how the other person makes us feel. You might say the same is true for romantic relationships, but choosing a partner is so much more complex, as our romantic choices often involve physical attraction, location, financial compatibility, job status, and so much more. We don't overthink making potential friends in the same way that we overthink connecting with romantic partners, and there's a beautiful 'ease' in that. That's not to say choosing and maintaining friendships is easy; selecting good friends requires a level of discernment, sociability and effort that may not come naturally to everyone. But when it comes to building a strong community, friendships are the best place to start.

I'm someone who has a relatively small circle. Outside of my family members, I can count my nearest and dearest friends on one hand, and I've been this way since I was a child. I've always had a 'best friend', and one or two close friends outside of this.

As I write, I am proud to say that my best friend has been my best friend for almost twenty years. I think this choice was heavily influenced by my parents – particularly my mother – because she is the same way. My mum always had a small number of friends while I was growing up. She is a very loyal person, who also has a good understanding of her likes and dislikes, so when she likes someone, and her relationship to them proves to be peaceful, respectful and mutually beneficial; she confides in and keeps them close.

My mum is also a very likeable person, who often attracts people who want to be her friend, and I consider myself quite similar to her in this way. I know I have the option to have plenty of friends, but I find comfort in having a handful, and like my mum, I choose this with the understanding that I can only give so much of myself to people. In my opinion, having many friends demands more energy from me, but at the same time, they'd then receive less effort from me because my energy must be distributed across several people.

With a more select number of friends, I can pour more into each of them – and in turn create deeper bonds. My mother feels very fulfilled in her friendships, and despite my similar small number of close friends, I share this sentiment – because what I lack in quantity, I make up for in deep and meaningful connections. I say this to highlight something very important: in building your soft community, you don't need a million friends. One or two very close friends with good character is enough to fill your cup.

So how do you go about building your soft community? In this chapter, I'm going to go over what makes a good friend, the type of red flags you should look out for and ways to make new connections in general.

Good Friends vs Bad Friends

It's all about energy

In 1993, Cambridge University Press published *Emotional Contagion*, by psychologist Elaine Hatfield and professors Richard Rapson and John Cacioppo. Their detailed investigation arose from Hatfield personally observing how her clients would present a shift in mood from simply being around certain people – especially people they were in close relationships with. Hatfield noticed this frequently, and decided to explore the phenomenon in more detail. She worked with colleagues to discover how other people can influence our own mood, and what they discovered was that in close relationships (romantic, familial and platonic), people unconsciously 'sync' with one another emotionally, and it's something that begins in our infancy.

For instance, have you ever looked at a baby and made a sad face before? Babies will often pout or even cry as a reaction to a sad expression seen on the face of a caregiver. Hatfield's study found that the facial expressions and physical movements of the company we keep transmit emotional signals to us and that these signals are then shared within groups, influencing collective behaviours and moods.

If you're wondering why I'm sharing this study with you, it's because I believe that on your journey to building community, the impact of other people's energy should be a key consideration. As someone who is big on energy myself, I not only pay attention to what people say but also *how* they say it. I'm also mindful of how I feel when I'm around certain people. Those with kind, happy and confident energy create happiness and confidence in me. In turn, people who are constantly negative only encourage me to take on those same negative emotions. Now that's not to say I don't have my own mind – because I most certainly do; but as the *Emotional Contagion* study highlighted, other people's behaviours and emotions can subconsciously influence our own, and it pays to be around people who transmit positive emotional signals to us.

To clarify, this doesn't mean my friends can't feel sad or low around me. Everyone has tough days, and it's totally normal to not be upbeat all the time. However, I personally try to lift myself up and stay positive, even when life gets stressful, and as a result I thrive around people who don't constantly carry a heavy or negative energy in their interactions.

Have you ever found yourself in the company of a negative friend? Perhaps you had a friend who was particularly pessimistic, judgemental or short-tempered? Think about how their energy rubbed off on you. Did you find yourself projecting similar emotions? How did that make you feel? It's worth reflecting on these experiences in your friendships.

Whether we want to admit it or not, our friends influence our mindset, and the company we choose to keep plays a major role in the quality of our life and general day-to-day feelings.

Choosing friends with the right energy isn't just about surrounding yourself with 'good vibes' – it's about protecting your nervous system and your peace.

The people around you will either help to regulate your emotions or trigger them, and when your circle is filled with friends who radiate joy, accountability and optimism, you begin to internalise that. Soft life isn't just about luxury or leisure – it's about living a life where your nervous system isn't perpetually anxious. Friends with positive energy allow you to breathe easy, and they help to make softness sustainable.

Supportiveness vs competitiveness

When competitiveness creeps into a friendship, it can be a red flag, because healthy friendships radiate support, not competition. Friendly competition amongst pals, which is built on a foundation of mutual encouragement, is fine. Sometimes we may compete with friends in a way that pushes both parties to try their very best and thrive. For example, in fundraising, sporting activities or any other activity built around competition, it's perfectly healthy to compete with friends in an uplifting or even playful way. However, sometimes you may find yourself in the presence of a 'friend' who competes with you out of a feeling of inferiority – which is typically a red flag.

The type of competitive friend you should be concerned about, chooses rivalry over support. Instead of celebrating your successes, they focus on 'who is doing better'. This leads them to regard your failure as a win. Competition in friendships often stems from insecurity. When someone struggles with low self-worth, another person's happiness or success can feel like a threat to theirs. They might constantly compare themselves and end up wanting to 'one-up' the people around them just to feel better. On the surface, a competitive friend might smile and even say all the right things, but their actions and energy tell a different story. Deep down, they may want you to do well, but not better than *them*. This subtle but significant red flag is important to look out for, and one way to notice it is to pay attention to a friend's enthusiasm when you succeed. A supportive friend is happily vocal or excited about your successes, but a competitive friend goes silent, quiet, or even changes the topic entirely when you bring up good news. And on the off-chance they do cheer for you, they may only ever do it in private, or in a way that might even minimise your achievements – like implying your success is a matter of luck or privilege, over talent or hard work. A competitive friend also attempts to downplay your successes by attempting to outdo you whenever you achieve something notable. If you tell them you backpacked through Cambodia, they did so through half of Asia; if you inform them that you ran a marathon in six hours, they allegedly did so in five.

On your journey to building your soft friendships, surround yourself with people who are encouraging and uplifting, and who understand that your success does not negate their own.

Good friends operate with the knowledge that your success is an indicator that success for them is also possible and, as such, they celebrate your wins and vice versa. In the eye of a good friend, personal timelines are not competitive. They view both your and their timelines as separate – because they understand that both journeys can exist, and flourish, side by side. They know that your wins don't equal losses for them, and they understand that your timing won't always match their timing, and that's OK.

Admiration vs envy

Envy is another red flag that is important to heed in friendships, because it's rooted in resentment. While competitiveness is rooted in a drive to succeed based on external or internal benchmarks, envy is tied to deep feelings of inadequacy. When a friend competes with you, they think 'I want to do better than them', but when a friend envies you, they think 'I want what you have, and I don't want you to have it.'

It is perfectly normal and acceptable to admire our friends. They may even influence our choices and decisions – from the material and superficial, to the impactful and meaningful. I've had friends who have changed their hairstyle to match mine because they liked how it looked on me and thought it might also look good on them. I've had friends who have influenced me to take social media more seriously, having witnessed the success they've personally had online. I've had friends who applied to certain companies because

I've previously worked there. That's not a problem. If anything, I think it's wonderful when you and your friends admire each other in a way that has a positive influence on everyone involved.

However, outside of harmless and endearing admiration, there's the type of admiration that is more sinister. The type that doesn't create room for co-existing but instead creates room for envy. The type that wants to be you in a way that desires your removal. A friend who desires your life doesn't want a job like yours – they want to take your job from you. A friend who wants your life doesn't desire a partner with the same values as yours – they want your partner. They do not wish to create their own life that mirrors the best parts of yours – they destructively and selfishly want to take what you've got. It's sinister when a friend wants to behave in this way, because healthy friendships cannot exist where sabotage lives. When a friend desires to replace you, or claim what is yours, they are no longer a friend, but an enemy. A real friend doesn't covet what you possess. If anything, they help you nourish and protect it, because they know it means something to you.

> It's vital for you to steer clear of people who wish to sabotage you, because in keeping them around, you will risk your happiness, your goals and your relationships with other people you care about.

To quote Oprah Winfrey, 'You can't be friends with anyone who wants your life.' In your community-building, embrace people who want the very best for others, with the understanding that it doesn't take away from their own possibilities. A good friend loves seeing their friends flourish at work, in their relationships and in their life generally. This is because a true friend finds joy in their friends' joy.

They do not wish to steal that joy. They do not wish to encroach on the life their friends have built for themselves in a way that disrupts it.

Secure attachment style vs possessiveness

When people discuss attachment styles, possessiveness, relationship anxiety and avoidance, it's often done in the context of romantic connections, but attachment styles show up in all relationship types. In the context of friendships, attachment style influences how people form bonds, how they handle conflict, and how someone copes when a friend becomes distant. For example, a good friend is a secure friend, who acknowledges that you have a life outside of them and encourages you to interact with other people – because they know that having a strong community comes with diversity.

A friend with healthy habits does not wish to suffocate you: they have a secure attachment style when it comes to their friendships. They understand the benefit of lived experiences with others, and the ways it can help you grow into a well-rounded person. The flip side of this is an anxious and possessive friend. I have had a possessive friend before, and during that time, I easily mistook her possessiveness for care. When someone wants to spend all their time with us, and wants to be our only point of community, we may view it as a reflection of deep love, however, much like possessive partners, possessive friends exude control disguised as love.

They want to control who you spend your time with and how you spend your time. The jealousy they have over your attention can even lead them to get upset if they see you developing closeness to others. The fear of abandonment that possessive friends have can prompt them to get in between your relationships with people, or even encourage you to damage your relationships with other friends. They may not respect your boundaries or even your space because of their desire to be attached to you.

Once the reality of this type of friendship comes to the surface, it can easily leave you feeling overwhelmed, isolated from others and anxious. Handling or stepping away from that dynamic takes clarity, boundaries and courage. You must pay attention to how your friend responds to you spending time with other people. Are they OK with it, or obviously upset? Do they guilt-trip you? Or suggest you are not invested in the friendship like them? Also, are they committed to your friendship in such a way that you feel uncomfortable or even suffocated?

If you notice this in a friendship, it's important that you administer boundaries, by redefining your friendship in a way that makes room for your peace, and for other people to exist alongside it. Redefining your friendship involves you not giving in to their tantrums or demands – by spending time with others, potentially reducing communication and voicing your discomfort. If the friendship doesn't evolve into a healthier dynamic, then it's important that you apply the courage to step away. The people who make up the soft community you choose to build should be able to co-exist with one another. This doesn't mean they have to be friends with each other outside of being friends with you, but they should understand that their friendship with you doesn't come with exclusivity. More importantly, soft friendships are nourishing, not draining.

If a friend is emotionally draining you by remaining possessive, you cannot exist in a state of softness within that dynamic. While softness in friendship doesn't require perfection (we are human after all), it does require a state of health, because when any relationship is not emotionally healthy, it is not soft.

Accountability

We can often make the mistake of believing that good friends should support us regardless of what we do. But the truth is, someone who supports you blindly isn't a good friend. Your community should also be able to hold you accountable when necessary.

Being a true friend to someone involves wanting the best for them, so when a good friend observes that you are doing things that go against your best interests and values, they challenge you. I don't expect blind support from my friends because I don't give them blind support.

> A friend who never calls you out, even when you're doing wrong, is a friend who enables you in the worst way – and if you want to flourish alongside your community, you should embrace and appreciate correction.

One major part of living softly, is showing up as the best version of ourselves – which is hard to do when we reject constructive criticism or advice. In order to grow, you need to be open to change, and to holding yourself and your friends accountable.

Small reminder: Holding someone accountable doesn't equate to being rude. When you're communicating something, consider your tone and communication style. A good friend knows how to challenge you and hold you accountable with kindness and compassion.

Summary

What makes a good friend? They:

- should be kind to you and others
- don't seek to compete with you in a way that celebrates your losses, because they want you to flourish
- celebrate your successes
- want you to have a life outside of them and recognise the importance of interacting with others
- do not attempt to control, belittle or speak badly about you
- encourage, uplift and want the best for you
- challenge you, with kindness and compassion, when you go against your best interests and values

Conversely, a bad friend:

- is constantly negative
- covets your life and wants to replace you so that they can have what you have
- wants you to do well but not better than them
- competes with you out of insecurity or envy
- is possessive and controlling of your time and attention

Your Community Reflects You

Jim Rohn was an American self-made millionaire, motivational speaker and author, who wrote several books on self-improvement. He also famously said that 'you are the average of the five people you spend the most time with'. To start with, I don't agree that our identity is shaped by just five people. I believe that our social networks in their entirety influence our identity – whether that's 10, 100 or 1,000 people. After all, a stay-at-home mum with three children, a husband and a nanny, isn't simply the average of her kids, husband and domestic support staff. In limiting our identity to an average of five people, we disregard the influence of all the people who came before them, and all the people outside of them. What's more, the impact of a connection does not always directly correlate to the frequency of that connection.

However, I do believe Jim Rohn was on to something. Successful and happy people are mindful about who they spend the most time with because they truly understand the impact of social networks. The company you keep can influence not just your emotions but also your ambitions, successes and safety. When you live by the theory that your 'key five' determines your outcomes, you are much more likely to be selective when choosing friends in general. Having a close friend who expresses a very pessimistic outlook, can easily influence you to view the world in a negative way. If that friend has quite self-limiting beliefs, and they project those beliefs onto you, you may even begin to doubt yourself and your own capabilities. Also, a friend who is controlling and possessive, may limit your ability to create new and impactful connections.

On the flip side, friends who express a positive outlook and an abundance mindset (see Chapter 4) can contribute to your personal and professional growth by encouraging you to chase your dreams, have faith in yourself and persevere in the face of adversity.

Good community can change the trajectory of your life.

I once read a BBC article titled, 'Want to live a long life? Start prioritising your friends'. It was written by award-winning journalist and author David Robson, and explored the role of friendship in maintaining good health. Robson, who is the author of *The Laws of Connection*, stated that 'our friendships can influence everything from our immune system's strength to our chances of dying from heart disease'. That if you want to live happily and healthily, prioritising community in the form of fostering friendships is important. Within the article, Robson noted a range of studies carried out across different decades – with one of them being an English Longitudinal Study of Ageing that involved 4,000 participants. The study found that higher loneliness levels predicted the onset of type two diabetes over the following decade, and that 'weak' community is also associated with a higher risk of dementia.

A separate 2006 study published in the *Journal of Clinical Oncology* found that women with strong community are more likely to survive breast cancer than those without. The researchers believed that this was due to community alleviating stress, which in turn boosts immune function. Outside of physical health, a lack of community is also linked to higher risks of depression – which is understandable, as loneliness and isolation is a major contributor to a range of mental health issues. To echo Robson's article, the impact of limited community on human beings may be why, in 2023, the World Health Organization went as far as launching a three-year initiative to address the global health threat that is posed by a lack of community.

Friendships have a powerful impact on our emotions, our health and our mental state. When people feel connected to a supportive network of friends, they tend to experience higher levels of happiness, improved emotional wellbeing, better health, and even a longer life expectancy. Your friends are so much more than people you simply 'spend time with'. They are a key component when it comes to knowing and feeling that you are living a fulfilled life – in other words, a soft life.

How to Cultivate Meaningful Friendships

At this point, you're probably thinking, 'It's all very nice knowing what makes a good friend versus a bad one, but how do I create my community in general?' When it comes to building community, one of the biggest pieces of advice I can give you is to be the type of friend you want to have. Attracting good friends isn't too different from attracting a good romantic partner. To appeal to the other person, you must possess character traits that are considered positive and endearing. In all my writing about good qualities and bad qualities, ask yourself whether you possess those good qualities. And if you acknowledge some of the bad ones within yourself, what are you going to do to tackle them?

Give space for meaningful conversations

As well as possessing good character, you need to be open to the idea of letting people in. If you're closed off to conversation, or against displaying any type of vulnerability, you will struggle to build community. Building connection and trust involves letting your guard down – even just slightly.

While small talk can be effective in the early stages of community-building, you will eventually need to engage in more meaningful conversations. You don't have to share every aspect of your life, but opening up just enough can be a gateway to building a bond, inviting mutual understanding and support, and helping people feel more comfortable around you through relatability. I've seen this first hand in my online community-building.

Despite having some of my social media accounts for over a decade, I didn't start developing any real kind of community until at least seven years in, because I had been too scared to be vulnerable. It was counter-productive. When I finally began opening up about my thoughts, my experiences, worries and more, my community began to grow and feel more supportive. In showing more of my 'real self', I made room for impactful connection – and creating in-person friends isn't much different.

Building community also involves self-reflection. Consider what makes a good friend and what makes a bad friend. Do you see any of those traits in yourself? If you possess many of the good traits I listed, you need to open up enough to share them with others. If you possess any of the bad traits, then the relationship building starts with you.

The first step is acknowledgement, and then being vulnerable with yourself. What triggers your desire to compete? What is the foundation of your envy? If you're a possessive friend, why do you cling on to others? Is it a fear of being abandoned? From there you can begin to work on your weaknesses – and do so with the understanding that this doesn't make you unworthy of friendship. You just need to do some self-work while you build those relationships.

Start with mutual interests

Another tip for building community is to start with mutual interests. Go wherever you may find like-minded individuals who are interested in similar things to you – whether that's via a sports club, music event, art class, travel, or more.

Shared activities create opportunities for natural connections to form, and being in an environment that is familiar to you can allow you to feel more relaxed. On the other hand, some people feel more confident in environments where they don't know anyone. If you're this type of person, it may pay you to diversify your social spaces.

Exploring new interests and friendships outside of your usual pool of people might help to make community-building seem less daunting, as the unfamiliarity may lead to fewer anxieties about being judged by peers or people you may run into day to day. In sharing mutual interests, it pays to be forthcoming and open. If someone asks you how you're enjoying a class, for example, don't just answer, 'Yeah, it's cool.' Replying with enthusiasm can make all the difference – 'I'm really enjoying it! It's my first time and I was a little nervous when it started, but everyone is really welcoming. Have you been coming often?' A response like this sends signals to others that you're open to conversing, getting to know them and making new friends.

Initiate

In building these connections, also consider initiating. The thought of initiating a conversation is daunting for many people – including myself – but I understand the power that comes with being willing to kick things off.

Initiation creates momentum because the connection-building is in your hands. There's no need to wait minutes, hours or days for someone to notice you or speak to you. When you initiate, you can get the ball rolling sooner rather than later. Initiating also invites connection, because people aren't mind readers. Many won't know you're open to making new friends or speaking to people in general, unless you signal that – and initiating conversation in social settings is a wonderful way to showcase approachability. If the pressure of potential in-person rejection concerns you, social media is also a great way to initiate new connections.

On social media you don't need to speak to any single individual if you feel nervous about doing so. Instead, you can put out a wider call as a status update, a story or a post. A simple 'looking to see if anyone who enjoys ____would be interested in checking out _____ on Saturday?' is enough to get the ball rolling, and from there you can filter accordingly.

Closing Thoughts

I'd be pretending if I said the process to building community will be seamless and free of rejection. You may find that in your attempt to make new friends, you aren't always successful – but that's part of any type of community-building. Not every connection will fit – and that's not a reflection of your value. Sometimes people just don't gel and that's OK. The more you try to build community, the more you will filter the people you gel with from the people you don't.

For those of you who already have good friends but want those relationships to feel more fulfilling, take the initiative to nurture these bonds. This can be as simple as checking in with a friend, making plans to spend time together, or simply expressing gratitude for their presence in your life. As you nurture your community, the main thing you must remember is to try and remain consistent, because it's that consistency that will build closeness and will help to ensure your community also consistently shows up for you.

Self-reflection prompts

What does your soft community currently look like?

Are there friends in your life who show red flags?

What sort of friend are you to others?

How long is your longest friendship?

Are there any green or red flags you recognise in yourself?

Do you struggle to make new friends, and if so, why?

What is your biggest weakness when it comes to making friends?

What steps have you identified you need to take to cultivate good friendships?

When was the last time you made a new friend, and how do you think that went?

MONEY EXPRESS
20

Soft Wealth: Spending with Intention is Self-Care

When people hear 'soft life', they often think of luxury – designer goods, spa days, opulent experiences and five-star living. But softness isn't simply about spending; it's about having freedom in whatever way you define it, and wealth is one of the most powerful ways we can create that freedom for ourselves. Wealth gives us options and provides us with a sense of security, but the softness of wealth is not about how much you can hustle, but rather, how much 'hustling' you can opt out of. It's not simply about acquiring things, but instead, feeling empowered to reclaim your life in a way that prioritises rest and peace.

Soft wealth is about freeing yourself from the rat race, from survival mode, from being at the mercy of someone else's priorities. It's about creating the type of wealth that enables you to build a life you don't feel the need to escape from.

In 2025 I briefly worked as a spokesperson for a widely recognised international bank. The bank had commissioned a report on 'the wealth perception gap', and my job was to talk to the media about the results of said report. I found the report fascinating because it highlighted how differently people view wealth in the UK.

Without getting into the specifics, what struck me was that people generally viewed wealth in one of two ways: material or non-material. For those who viewed wealth as material, being 'wealthy' was defined by earning six plus figures a year and having a kitchen island. For those who viewed wealth as non-material, it was about being in good health, and having the freedom to work anywhere, anytime. I personally didn't perceive either stance to be wrong. After all, as highlighted in the report, our perception of wealth is influenced by a range of factors – including our age, gender, income, race and geographical location. But I do think there's something to be said about assessing wealth holistically – because what's all the money in the world if we're not healthy enough to spend it? What's all the money in the world if we don't have the freedom to use it?

Is Wealth Really Just About Numbers?

Before I go into what wealth means to me, I'm first going to break down a few perceptions of wealth, beginning with the traditional mindset. Traditionally, wealth was mostly defined in financial and material terms – how much money you have in the bank, the net worth of your assets, social markers like the type of car you drive, the clothes you wear or the neighbourhood you live in. Wealth was (and for many people still is) about numbers, and numbers alone. This mindset can be limiting, even deceptive. It often reduces a fulfilling life to possessions, while ignoring the unseen costs – such as burnout, chronic stress, isolation, or even broken relationships. In today's world, the definition of wealth is evolving, which is vital for our survival.

> True wealth doesn't add money to the bank while deducting years from our lifespan. Nor does it grant us access to expensive things while diminishing our access to peace of mind.

True wealth is increasingly being viewed as good health, freedom to roam and time to do the things you enjoy.

Health is wealth

In 2011, co-founder of Apple, Steve Jobs, passed away following his battle with pancreatic cancer – an aggressive cancer with one of the lowest five-year survival rates. Jobs died with an estimated net worth of $7 billion dollars. He was just 56 years old at the time of his death. One might argue that Steve Jobs was the very definition of 'wealthy'. After all, he had 'made it' internationally, and even reached multi-millionaire status by his twenties. However, at his most unwell, it's not preposterous to think that Jobs would have likely traded in all his money for good health if he could have.

Financial wealth means very little when people are in extremely ill health. Sure, money can grant you access to better treatment and better drugs and the most expensive consultants, but there are many illnesses that money simply can't cure.

Despite being one of the richest men of his time, Warren Buffett often advocated for prioritising health – using analogies to get the message across. To paraphrase some advice he once gave to students, *imagine being given a car and it's the only car you will have for the rest of your life. With this knowledge, you will treat it with care, and service it regularly*. This is how Buffett states you should treat your mind and body, because after all, it is the only mind and body you will ever have.

The fact of the matter is, when we speak about health in financial terms, ill health is expensive. In fact, ill health is probably one of the most expensive things in the world – because it can cost you your peace, wellbeing, life savings and even your life itself. As such, one of the best investments you can make is not in stocks or shares, or a business. It's investing in your body.

Your time is your currency

Beyond ill health, another very costly thing is time. Time is particularly costly because we can't create it. All we can do is spend it. Once it's gone, there's no getting it back. For this reason, when we review wealth holistically, I think it's safe to say money is one type of wealth, but another type of wealth is time, and the freedom to control your own time.

As well as good health, time allows you to be present with the people you love, it gives you the freedom to rest, and it allows you to explore who you are beyond simply working. That's why freedom of time is such a powerful part of living softly – because it frees you from obligations and commitments that drain you. Having free time means you can take charge of your life and invest in moments that are meaningful, memorable and peaceful. In fact, you may argue that having free time is as important as having good health because when your time belongs to you, you're rarely in a state of panic, anxiety or hyper-productivity. Free time empowers us to simply exist. It's a privilege that reduces stress and creates room to build connections and enjoy life's little moments. Simply put, being a multi-millionaire who is glued to a computer screen for 50 hours a week, is far from living softly. But living without significant financial worries, with the ability to wake up when you feel like it, sleep when you want, and travel when you desire is certainly more in keeping with soft living.

Wealth and Soft Living

So now that we've looked at a holistic approach to wealth, let's talk about building finances based on your priorities and what wealth personally means to you. You may be thinking, 'If monetary wealth is about excess and abundance, how does this truly align with soft living?' After all, earning large amounts of money usually means working hard for it. The constant chase for more is often tied to hustle culture, long hours and burnout, because most millionaires didn't just stumble into money – they worked for it, and many worked relentlessly.

When it comes to attaining wealth while living softly, first, it's important to be mindful of the psychological and physical impact of wealth-building. Even in my own work, I must choose sustainability over speed of financial growth, to avoid burnout. I know that working twelve hours a day is unsustainable for me, so I don't do it. Could I potentially get more done and make more money if I worked longer hours? Perhaps. But I also know that in stretching myself I reduce my efficiency and creativity, so I do enough to produce consistently high-quality work without wrecking my wellbeing. I also prioritise work based on the biggest returns. I never try to do everything all at once. Instead, I say yes to the most impactful things, and I prioritise them according to whether they will be quick wins or big wins. I also set clear goals surrounding what wealth means to me.

The Rest-Rich Method

As appealing as the big house, flashy car and fancy clothes might be – possessing material wealth is not important to me if it means compromising my freedom or health in the process. What grounds me is something I now call the Rest-Rich Method.

It begins with a simple question: *What does 'enough' look like to me?*

Knowing my personal threshold prevents me from wearing myself out and chasing excess out of fear, ego or keeping up with the Joneses. I don't run myself ragged and burn out striving for things I don't actually need. Don't get me wrong – I see the appeal of attaining certain social markers of wealth, but experience has taught me that material wealth means very little if it comes at the cost of my peace, time, health, and overall wellbeing.

Coming to that realisation didn't happen overnight though. I had to go through the rat race, the exhaustion and the materialism to finally understand that, for the most part, it just isn't worth the struggle. When I was at my most stressed and overworked, I had to return to the drawing board and consider when I felt grounded and calm. The truth was that overworking didn't add to my peace – it disrupted it. Yes, it put a little extra money in the bank, but at what cost? It wasn't enough to justify the stress I was experiencing.

In the end, I had to reflect on the end goal – what was I even chasing and why? At my busiest, I had no monetary amount in mind, or financial goal I wanted to reach – I just wanted 'more', without actually understanding what that looked like. Why did I want more? It wasn't because I was deeply unhappy with what I already had, but because I thought I was supposed to achieve more – largely due to comparing myself to others and giving in to the societal expectations that dictate what success looks like as a twenty-something.

In my mind, the harder you worked, the more money you made, and the more money you made, the better off you were, *right?* Not necessarily. If you're a rap fan, you may know that The Notorious B.I.G. once famously said 'Mo Money, Mo Problems'. I can see how that can be true when a person only makes money through mentally and physically pushing themselves in ways that are draining. The truth is, I am most fulfilled when I have time to think, rest and create without pressure. And I feel depleted when I over-extend myself in the name of status. In my thirties, I decided to define my 'enough' – not in a way that limited me, but in a way that protected my softness. And do you know what was most ironic about that? In prioritising my freedom and creativity, I created, and in creating, I found purpose, and my purpose attracted money.

When my wellbeing took priority, everything else seemed to fall into place – which makes sense because, after all, how productive can you truly be when you are mentally and physically depleted?

I want to help you to determine your 'enough' in three easy steps:

Step 1: Take Note of Your Energy

I want you to keep a record of when you feel most at peace and most happy. What energises you? Is it painting, writing, spending time with other people? What makes you feel most alive? Might it be travelling, or completing a sporting activity? And what drains you? Maybe that answer could even be one of the examples I've already given.

Step 2: Define Your 'Enough'

What do you need to feel secure? Are there any things you cannot compromise or negotiate on? What would you do less of if you felt that you had nothing to prove? What would you do more of if you felt that nobody was judging you? Is there a monetary amount that you feel would enable you to live in a way that fulfils you? When I personally answered these questions, it emphasised how much I love travel. It helped me determine that being able to travel frequently was one of my 'enoughs', and having enough money to do that was very important to me.

Step 3: Define Your Work Boundaries

Based on your answers, define the things you want to stop doing, and the things you want to start. At the time I considered all of this, I was working a 9–5 job and made the decision to leave it once I felt that I was making 'enough' money from my creative work to meet my basic needs. Maybe you don't have the luxury of leaving your job entirely, but your boundary could look like not working past 5 p.m., or saying 'no' to work that is not your responsibility. In determining your 'enough', you need to set limits when life demands more than you're open to giving.

Building Wealth

Financial literacy

In reading all of the above, what does wealth look like to you? Do you see wealth in non-material ways, like health, time and freedom – or is acquiring material things still very important to you? Whatever your answer, I'd be pretending if I said money doesn't play any part whatsoever. Money still plays a role. How *much* money you feel you need, is tied to your 'enoughs', but let's look into how we can get access to whatever it is we need.

If you've ever read books about acquiring wealth, you will know that the advice remains fairly consistent. Financial literacy is typically at the forefront of the advice, because it's very hard to manage and grow what you don't understand. For many people, financial literacy was unfortunately not taught to them in school, since the expectation is that it is learned at home. Sadly, not everyone is raised in a household where financial literacy is taught, or even talked about. As first-generation immigrants, my parents didn't know much about how Western financial systems worked. Growing up, I noticed that much of their learning was by trial and error – largely because when they were in their twenties, living in eighties Nigeria, credit cards weren't a thing. Cash was king and therefore most Nigerians knew nothing about credit.

When we moved to the UK in the nineties, information wasn't particularly easy for them to access because they had no idea what to look out for. They made decisions based on sheer desperation, or the little information they received, and sometimes those decisions would backfire. For example, ordering through catalogues while not acknowledging interest rates, or renting a television simply due to not being able to afford it outright. This resulted in them paying much more towards things than necessary, and having little to no disposable income sometimes.

I often felt frustrated as a child, confused as to why we had to shop in charity stores, and why my peers seemed to have much more than I did. At the time I thought my parents were just broke, without considering the hurdles they faced that so many of my peers' parents didn't – like uprooting their entire life from one country to another with very little money. But thankfully, as my parents learned about finances, I did too – including learning from their mistakes.

I knew that my parents would have made different decisions had they had access to more tools, so I made sure to make the most of the tools I had access to – whether that was through reading books or watching videos on social media. With time, they also learned to do the same thing. I'm by no means a financial expert, but I feel confident that I will be able to teach my future children the money lessons I never got growing up. Thanks to a lot of self-teaching, I've built strong financial habits and even have an excellent credit score to show for it. I'm sharing this to say, even if you didn't grow up learning about money, it's never too late to start. There are endless resources, books, videos and podcasts available – you just have to take advantage of them.

Financial literacy

In taking advantage of what was available to me, I noticed frequent messaging surrounding the benefits of having multiple income streams. In all the books I read and the videos I watched, I was reminded that most millionaires didn't make their money doing only one thing – they had multiple jobs, multiple businesses and investments, or all of the above. I made sure to monetise the things I was comfortable making money from, so I could acquire wealth using different skills and in different ways.

With that said, work–life balance was and still is important to me – and in considering my 'enough', I had to review what I enjoy doing and what I hate doing. I knew I love sharing my thoughts, and writing was a key part of my brand – so my work as an author was not up for negotiation. I also enjoy speaking and it rarely feels like 'work' to me – so I advertised myself as a speaker, registering for paid speaking websites, and I also took up panel opportunities.

Content creation also comes very naturally to me. If I wasn't paid to create content, I would still create it – because I love taking photos and recording videos and I enjoy online discourse. I knew that content creation and working with brands was a strong income stream which I wanted to continue for as long as I could. I took my love of speaking, and my love of content, and launched a podcast with the help of an amazing team – which also contributed to further income.

The key point I want to emphasise is that despite having four streams of income, I rarely feel drained by my work, because it excites and invigorates me, and I sincerely enjoy it. That's not to say it doesn't get stressful sometimes – even when you enjoy what you do, it can be overwhelming. But I try my best to assert my boundaries.

If you're thinking about how to grow your income streams, my first bit of advice is to **build a strong foundation**. Before I started branching out, my foundation was my work as a content creator. I did my best to master that single stream of income first, and then tapped into others. My work as a creator also helped me to build my personal brand – and in building that brand I was able to tap into further opportunities like the writing, speaking and podcasting. For some people, their foundation is their 9–5 job, but if you want a different foundation and you're not sure about where to start, consider where your strengths lie. What are your skills and interests, and how can you monetise them? Perhaps you can teach, consult, or sell your own work? It's helpful to monetise what you're skilled at, rather than start from scratch. Once you have your foundation secured, then you can explore alternative income opportunities. Many of the books I read highlighted the value in generating passive income, i.e., money you earn with minimal ongoing effort once the initial 'heavy lifting' has been completed. Examples of passive income include royalties from books or music, earnings from digital product sales, dividends from investments, rental income and affiliate marketing. The work is done upfront, but eventually money can be made with little to no ongoing daily effort. I imagine you can guess what my current passive income is... You're reading one of the producers of it right now.

Scarcity vs abundance mindset

Another key component for building wealth (according to the experts) **is shifting your mindset from a scarcity mindset to one of abundance.** Whether it is *Think and Grow Rich* by Napoleon Hill, *Rich Dad, Poor Dad* by Robert Kiyosaki or *Secrets of the Millionaire Mind* by T. Harv Eker, one message ties all these books together: possessing an abundance mindset is vital for building financial wealth.

But what is an abundance mindset? It's the belief that money is accessible and available. Someone who has an abundance mindset believes that there is enough money to go round and that with the right effort, they can make a lot of it. They believe that even though money comes and goes, when it goes, it will return. Someone with a scarcity mindset, however, has strong money anxieties and believes that there is a lack of available money, and that if it goes, it may not necessarily come back.

You might be thinking, 'Why is having an abundance mindset crucial for making money?' Well, people who believe that money is everywhere are more willing to take risks – like pumping their money into a business or making certain investments which could prove lucrative. They are also more open to considering ways to grow or invest their money, because unlike someone with a scarcity mindset, they do not hoard or believe they will struggle to make more of it. In addition, they function in a state of gratitude and not a state of deprivation – and according to the likes of Hill, Kiyosaki and Eker, this influences financial outcomes, because we amplify what we focus on, and putting our energy into gratitude only attracts more opportunities for gratitude in our lives.

Closing Thoughts

Wealth does not have one single definition. If anything, it's personally defined by what we want to get out of life. We all have different priorities and share different values, and as a result, we all view wealth differently. Your definition of wealth doesn't have to look like everyone else's. While many people define wealth in material terms, wealth doesn't have to be defined by you in the same way. For you, it might not look like a six-bedroom mansion in the Hollywood Hills. It may look like good health, free time, no debts and freedom. For others it may look like a Ferrari and a penthouse in London. The beauty of it is being able to define it for ourselves.

> A huge part of soft living is not following the crowd but instead, defining life on your terms, and putting your values at the centre.

I feel wealthy in life – not because I am rich, but because I possess everything I need and want. I have a roof over my head, food in my stomach, no crippling debt, a strong and loving community and fulfilment in my work; I am healthy, and I can do things that I enjoy. The wealth I possess is a product of not just my own personal efforts in building my dream life, but also my willingness to find contentedness.

The thing about the material pursuit of wealth is that it often never ceases. American businessman and philanthropist John D. Rockefeller was once asked 'How much money is enough?' Rockefeller famously replied 'Just a little bit more.' Despite being one of the wealthiest people in human history, Rockefeller proved that the desire for more never really stops when we reduce wealth to material things alone. In your quest for wealth, you must define your 'enough'. You must learn contentment. When you define wealth on your own terms, you can pursue it without losing your health, freedom or yourself in the process.

Self-reflection prompts

What does wealth currently mean to you?

Are there any social markers of wealth that you feel that you want, and why?

Would you say you have a positive or negative relationship with money?

Now that you've read this chapter, how has your perception of wealth changed?

Who taught you about money, and what did they teach you that sticks in your mind?

What steps can you take to build up your financial literacy?

Have you ever considered additional streams of income?
What might they look like?

How much money is enough for you?

Soft Boundaries: You Are Not Here to Please Everyone

Sometimes being disliked is an indicator that you're doing something right. On your journey to creating your soft life, it is almost guaranteed that you will run into hurdles along the way.

One of the biggest challenges with redefining life for many people comes with recalibrating their habits, routines and former processes. Interestingly, it's not actually initiating the recalibration that feels most difficult... The hardest part is dealing with what other people will have to say – especially if they aren't used to you implementing boundaries or asking for what you want.

The Importance of Asserting Boundaries

I believe many of the problems people (particularly women) face in life, stem from a difficulty with asserting boundaries. Gender expectations and social conditioning mean that from an early age, women are typically taught to prioritise likeability, 'keeping the peace' and taking care of others, over meeting their own needs. To many people, a man saying 'no' is a symbol of assertiveness, whereas a woman saying 'no' is often painted as cold, unkind, difficult, ungrateful or 'high-maintenance'.

In fact, a 2022 Pew Research Center report found that 77 per cent of women say they feel pressure to be accommodating, even when it goes against what they actually want. A separate 2009 study published in *Psychology of Women Quarterly* found that women are also more likely than men to experience guilt when they do finally assert their own needs.

Whether it's from burnout, anxiety or stress, an inability to create or assert boundaries influences not just how people treat us but also the hurdles we face and the burdens we carry.

Speaking up and saying no

Learning to create boundaries, vocalise your wants and simply say 'no', are some of the most important things you can do for yourself on your journey to making life feel less challenging.

We all know women who say 'yes' to almost everything, and from my account of my past, I'm sure you know that I was one of those people. They're the mothers, aunties and sisters who are burned out due to providing excessive amounts of emotional, physical or financial labour. And they're the female colleagues who take on other people's responsibilities – remaining at work to complete tasks, when they should have clocked out.

Society further encourages women to over-extend themselves by labelling selfless women as 'strong', as if dismissing your own needs is a badge of honour. Reclaiming the right to say 'no' is a radical act because in reclaiming your energy, time and life, you are sticking a middle finger up at the societal expectation that women should always 'make time' for others.

Pulitzer Prize-winning historian Laurel Thatcher Ulrich famously said 'well-behaved women seldom make history'. Ulrich aimed to highlight how history overlooks women who quietly follow social rules, and in my opinion, there is a reason for this. Living as a woman who subscribes to society's expectations of what a woman should be, seems to involve being 'seen and not heard', being 'pleasant' even when you have no desire to be, following instead of leading, and dulling yourself to make room for men. It's difficult to have any type of impact when you are living like this and, furthermore, it's difficult to be happy and live softly when you are diminishing aspects of your personality to fit a box society has created for you.

Living softly relies on living authentically, and a large part of this process requires being truly honest with yourself and others about your wants, needs and dislikes.

From a young age, girls are typically taught to be accommodating. As a woman, the prioritisation of other people's needs over your own is viewed as an endearing norm, but it only makes it harder for young women to set boundaries or make requests. For a long time, I struggled with vocalising my wants – in both a personal and professional context. I spent most of my twenties trying to be 'agreeable', because I believed that is how women should be, but it only made my life harder, not softer.

So, what happens when a woman asserts a need or desire, or implements a boundary? It's viewed by some as a social abnormality, and by default, she is viewed as socially problematic – which is often why women are pushed into a state of agreeableness. If you can relate to this, you're not alone. Studies have found that whilst women are typically better than men at communicating relationship needs, we often struggle more than men with communicating work and career needs.

I've certainly struggled with this in the past. When I started working as a full-time creator, I would often be asked what my rate was, and would find myself feeling too nervous to request what I truly wanted.

If anything, I would present a lesser rate out of fear of being judged harshly or appearing greedy.

A 2003 study titled 'Women Don't Ask: Negotiation and the Gender Divide', by Linda Babcock and Sara Laschever, examined whether a difference exists between men and women in their approach to initiating salary negotiations. The study involved a range of experiments, surveys and interviews involving male and female job seekers, corporate professionals and MBA students. It found that men are up to four times more likely than women to negotiate for higher salaries – citing social conditioning, fear of backlash and lack of encouragement as reasons why many women may avoid negotiating.

Negotiations surrounding money can often feel daunting and somewhat confrontational, going against how society dictates women should behave. When you have been taught to be accommodating – even when it doesn't serve you – you can hesitate when asking for anything that you believe may inconvenience someone else, since a 'gracious' and 'accommodating' woman accepts what she is given.

In not accepting, women might feel as if they are being disruptive – linking back to the 2009 *Psychology of Women Quarterly* suggesting women feel guilt when asserting their needs. The hesitation by women to negotiate for higher salaries may also be due to a feeling of imposter syndrome – i.e., believing you are a fraud, underqualified and therefore undeserving. Or it could even be due to self-doubt.

Years ago, I shared a post online about a popular and widely cited Hewlett-Packard report that investigated the differing rates of job applications by men and women. The report found that men typically apply for jobs when they meet 60 per cent of the criteria. Women, on the other hand, usually apply when they meet 100 per cent. The post went viral – because many people believed the results accurately highlighted a key problem in society.

While I understand that there are many systemic issues at play regarding gender inequality in work and business, we can't disregard the fact that for many women, low confidence and a lack of audacity is also a major barrier towards them getting what they desire, and this is largely due to how women are socialised. When you've spent years dulling, silencing and shrinking yourself to be liked, you become hyper conscious of not coming across as too loud, too sure of yourself, and too 'seen'. You end up watering down your needs, dismissing your goals and denying yourself to make others feel comfortable. This inevitably bites you in the butt, because in holding yourself back, you are subconsciously convincing yourself that you are not worthy to take up space. You end up denying yourself freedom and living inauthentically.

Over time, this constant self-monitoring only feeds self-doubt, further imposter syndrome, and the quiet belief that your strengths are a flaw. The truth is, fear of being seen doesn't help us as women – it only limits us, and the longer we live in fear of having 'audacity', the more we risk never manifesting our potential.

> On your quest to living softly, your job is not to be liked by everyone – it's to be liked by yourself and those who matter to you.

The Cambridge Dictionary defines audacity as 'courage or confidence of a kind that other people find shocking or rude'. But

I personally believe that we need to stop viewing audacity as an entirely negative thing.

To achieve your dream soft life, you will sometimes need to shock people, and you will need to take on challenges that require you to display the type of courage or confidence others may find uncomfortable.

People often find audacity unpalatable because it can manifest as an expression of selfishness and a complete disregard for others. However, that's not the only type of audacity that exists. Audacity can also come in the form of taking up space or making yourself heard in an environment that typically doesn't consider you, or asking for things that are believed to be out of reach for you. Like asking for an opportunity when you're new in a role, not because you've spent years working up to it, but because you believe in your heart that despite your newness, you have what it takes to smash it. Audacity can come in the form of making a cold call, because you believe that you have more to gain than to lose.

Learning to be confident in yourself and your capabilities boosts your willingness to be audacious – and that willingness will get you far. Who cares if you only meet seven out of ten requirements on a job profile – apply anyway. Maybe you can learn on the job? Maybe you can outsource? If you believe you can do the job regardless, then go for it.

Audacity can get you very far because with it you no longer wait for permission but you go for what you want unapologetically. In being audacious, you may build relationships that could change your life, you may land opportunities that you once thought were out of reach, you may shock or surprise people in a way that earns their respect. Sometimes displaying audacity is the bridge between you living your dream life and staying stuck where you are. However, it may also result in you being disliked by people who don't possess the courage to display that same level of audacity.

Women may hesitate with asserting boundaries or asking for what they want, out of a fear of dislike and backlash, which is quite understandable. For generations, women who have disrupted the status quo or leaned into their voice, have often been met with exclusion, criticism or even punishment – think Rosa Parks refusing to give up her seat on a bus, Greta Thunberg calling out world leaders over climate inaction, Tarana Burke facing backlash after starting the #MeToo movement... We've been conditioned to silence ourselves as much as possible, so when we do speak up, we know that it often comes at a cost.

Facing the Backlash

A 2001 study titled 'Prescriptive gender stereotypes and backlash toward agentic women' (agentic meaning those with agency to express their needs and goals) examined how gender stereotypes affect how people perceive women who display behaviours suggesting they have agency. The investigation by social psychologists Laurie Rudman and Peter Glick, helped coin the term 'the backlash effect', as it was (unsurprisingly) noted that women who demonstrate confidence, assertiveness and a clear sense of autonomy, typically face a backlash. Why, you might ask? Because they are said to violate societal gender norms suggesting women should be more submissive.

The emotional toll of this is real, with many women feeling punished, not for failing, but for excelling. It's so sad to think that when women make a conscious effort to be more confident, speak up and stand up for themselves, they are sometimes disliked for it. I would even go as far as to say that some women also internalise this belief... Have you ever heard a woman say that she hates working under other women? When your fellow woman isn't fond of you expressing your agency, it's no surprise that you might desire being liked over being assertive.

As a woman, being assertive can certainly feel isolating, because as the study highlighted, with increased competence comes less likeability... This is something I experienced on my own journey towards living a softer life. The more I vocalised my opinion, asserted boundaries and made it clear that I possess the ability, knowledge and skill to write and speak effectively, the more 'unlikeable' I became to certain people – mostly men.

Unfortunately, many men believe women should be passive, and when a woman goes against the 'submissive ideal', she's often viewed as a threat to the patriarchy – a system built by men for their own personal gain.

The rise of incel culture has emboldened a terrifying number of men to view female autonomy as a problem. We're living in a time where young men are acquiring advice from older men who possess deeply engrained hatred for women. Violence against women and girls is on the rise, with the World Health Organization stating that 1 in 3 women worldwide (i.e., about 736 million) have experienced physical and/or sexual violence in their lifetime. Women's rights are being rolled back globally – think of the 2022 decision to overturn *Roe v. Wade* (abortion rights) in the United States or the elimination of women's access to education in Afghanistan. These examples are just a couple among many, and they reflect a wider pushback against the progress and autonomy of women – often under the guise of 'tradition', 'morality', and/or religion.

Unfortunately for the men who had issues with me expressing my own autonomy, I knew that for things to change for the better in my life, I had to be stricter with the way I operated. I had to vocalise my wants, my disdain, my annoyances, and I had to stop being afraid of the potential backlash that would come with my speaking my mind, saying 'no' to people, or asking for what I truly desired. The more fulfilled I became with my life, the more I was viewed as 'high maintenance', 'problematic' and 'unaccommodating'. But in feeling more fulfilled, I can't say that I cared about this shift in perception, because the reward far outweighed the backlash for me.

My personal experience is just one example of women being disliked for being vocal, assertive or confident – but the fact is, we see this type of backlash play out all the time in business, politics, sport and entertainment.

Another example is tennis player Serena Williams, who participated in the US Open in 2018, and made headlines not for her athleticism but for vocalising her annoyance at an umpire over unfair treatment. Serena's actions were not uncommon to see in the tennis world – particularly amongst male players – yet she was labelled 'aggressive', highlighting a clear double standard in sports. Had she not been a woman, or a Black woman at that, her response would arguably have been considered part and parcel of the game.

Similarly, the likes of Hillary Clinton and Kamala Harris have been dubbed 'too calculating' for being considered, or 'unlikeable' for being assertive. Meghan Markle, who set boundaries with the British press and royal family, went on to face a tirade of further abuse and was labelled 'manipulative', 'controlling' and 'difficult', simply for asserting those boundaries with the goal of preserving her wellbeing.

If you are a woman who is implementing a boundary, vocalising a dislike or demonstrating assertiveness, there will be people who will dislike you for it, because they believe women should always be accommodating.

Some people will also dislike you just because your presence reminds them of something they lack or wish they had. You might trigger an insecurity, not by anything you've done to them, but simply by being yourself. Instead of dealing with their own feelings, these individuals will choose to project them onto you. The only way to make people like this feel comfortable is to shrink yourself – but that will only deplete you over time.

People's personal comfort shouldn't come at the cost of your confidence, your successes, your blessings or your skills.

There is no satisfactory way to win over someone like this. You must accept that they dislike you and live authentically regardless, because the alternative is dimming yourself, and people-pleasing to the point of living in long-term unhappiness.

You may also run into people who dislike you because your personalities simply don't gel – and that's OK. They may find you too loud, too shy, too direct, too emotional, too choosy, etc. Not every personality meshes, not every sense of humour aligns, and not every person will click with you. Problems will arise if you try to force connection, earn approval or change yourself to be liked.

The reality is, on your journey to creating a softer life, you will be misunderstood, judged or disliked by some people – no matter how kind or considered you are. One of the most powerful forms of freedom is having the confidence to be disliked, especially if you've been programmed to people-please. When your worth has been tied to receiving validation from others, being disliked can feel like a personal failure, but the truth is being liked by everyone often comes at the cost of being fully yourself.

If you can't live authentically, you're wearing a mask, and that isn't aligned to living softly. Soft living shouldn't be hard, limiting or pretentious – it should be honest and easy.

If someone doesn't like you, hold your head up regardless, with the knowledge that you are living in your truth. Being accepted by yourself is the most powerful form of acceptance, and what matters more than whether people like you, is whether *you* like *yourself*.

Acceptance

This leads me on to the main takeaway of this chapter... Not everyone will like you, and that's OK.

Do you know which kind of person is loved by many? The people pleaser.

The people pleaser is a person who has a compulsive desire to satisfy other people, frequently prioritising the feelings and needs of others above their own. It's a behaviour that is driven by a need for validation and a fear of conflict. People pleasers struggle to say 'no', invalidate their own emotions and thoughts, rarely assert boundaries, over-apologise, and constantly seek approval from others. Being a people pleaser is the antithesis of someone who lives a soft life, because their life is guided not by what they want to get out of it, but by how everyone else around them feels and views them.

Now in saying all this, I'm not suggesting you should aim to be disliked by everyone you cross paths with. I pride myself on being well-mannered, kind and respectful. However, I'm no longer in the business of trying to be liked by everybody, because I understand that in catering to everyone, I cannot cater to myself. And to live my dream life, I need to make myself one of my biggest priorities – by setting boundaries, vocalising my wants and learning to say no.

Here are the three rules I live by to put myself first:

1. Set boundaries

I touched on the importance of setting boundaries when I spoke about self-love, but the truth is, I can't stress it enough. Before a boundary is initiated, it should exist in your mind. Write down your non-negotiables and consider the boundaries that match them. For example, people respecting my space is a non-negotiable for me. I will therefore not tolerate someone invading my personal space without consent, or using my things without asking – and should they do so, I will assert my boundary. Which leads me on to how you communicate boundaries. Some people share their boundaries proactively; other times people share their boundaries only if and when they've been crossed. Think about how you will let people know something is a boundary for you, and how you will reinforce it. A clear boundary could look like having a lock on your door, or simply even having a conversation.

2. Vocalise your wants

When you have the conversations, be honest and firm – without being unkind. Advocate for yourself in a way that allows no room for confusion. If you want something, make that clear – without sounding like the other person is doing you a favour or you are inconveniencing them. Don't hinder yourself waiting for the 'perfect time' either. It's often better to address something in the moment than to leave it to fester and bring it up when it's no longer relevant.

3. Learn to say no

When it comes to saying no, it pays to be direct. 'I don't think so', and 'maybe not' won't cut it. Say it how it is. But what you mustn't do is fall into the trap of over-apologising once you've made your stance clear. Setting boundaries and speaking up won't come to you overnight. Practice makes perfect. If you struggle, start with saying 'no' to small things, and work your way up. The more you allow yourself to say 'no', the more you will feel comfortable with sharing exactly how you feel.

One of my favourite musicals is *Hamilton*. Admittedly, before the show, I knew very little about Alexander Hamilton's life. In fact, I knew just two things – that he was one of the founding fathers of the United States, and that he is credited with saying that 'those who stand for nothing fall for anything' – though opinions are divided as to whether he really did say this or not. Whoever it was, I think this quote is an important one for you to remember on your journey to living your soft life.

Standing for something, whether it's honesty, self-respect, your boundaries or your personal aspirations, helps you build real confidence and attract people who truly align with you. A great example of this type of woman is Malala Yousafzai. Malala is best known for her activism work – more specifically, defending girls' education in Pakistan, despite death threats from the Taliban. In fact Malala was seen as such a threat to the regime's agenda that they attempted to assassinate her. In 2012, she was shot by a Taliban gunman on her way home from school, but thankfully, she survived, and despite the assassination attempt, she continued to fight for what she believed in. Two years later, at the age of just 17, she became the youngest person to be awarded a Nobel Peace Prize.

Malala deviated from the social norms that required her to shrink herself. She understood that the cost of being 'liked' was her autonomy, her voice, her truth, her ambition, and the future of so many young girls just like her. Malala didn't desire being liked. She desired happiness, and she knew that the only way for her to attain that was through attaining freedom and being true to herself.

You may think that it pays to be agreeable, and that 'soft living' is about living a zero-conflict life of emotional and mental ease. But when you don't have a clear sense of your own values, boundaries or beliefs, you'll easily be swayed by what others want, think and expect.

If you want to live a soft life (particularly as a woman), understand that your personal fulfilment shouldn't be tied to public opinion. If you allow public opinion to dictate your choices and actions, you will never be satisfied, because societal standards call for women to dull themselves. Use my words as a reminder that constantly trying to be liked by everyone can cause you to lose your sense of self.

I remember a time when I hated conflict. The mere thought of someone having a problem with me would create a knot in my stomach. Even when I felt as if I was in the right, I couldn't bear facing conflict head on – which meant I didn't do the best job at advocating for myself, and often felt as if other people were controlling my life.

When you're focused on avoiding conflict or gaining approval, you may agree with things you don't believe in, say yes when you mean no, or change who you are just to fit in. Requiring constant approval leads you down a path of self-suppression, and over time it can leave you feeling disconnected, resentful and unsure of who you really are. This can leave you standing for nothing.

Even in a soft life, conflict is inevitable, because in choosing yourself, you won't always choose others, and that may annoy some people. But managing conflict softly looks like choosing grace over aggression, and peace over chaos. The goal isn't to avoid conflict altogether, but to approach it in a way that is controlled, regulated and still makes room for you to uphold your character and peace.

As I was navigating how to get better at dealing with conflict, I discovered that for me, chasing clarity was one great way – because what is often viewed as conflict may just be miscommunication. In addition, I stopped meeting people at the level they present to me. I meet people at the level I am comfortable with. If someone is shouting at me, it's stressful for me to shout back. Instead, I maintain my power and control by talking at a volume and pace that I am OK with. I also use language that aligns with my values. I do not use attacking language because it doesn't promote a resolution, and nor does it align with my character. Instead, I focus primarily on getting my point across with respect and clarity. A large part of managing conflict also involves knowing when to end the conversation. Not everyone is owed a response and not everyone deserves your energy.

> The most fulfilled people in our society have accepted being disliked. To live softly you must release yourself from the opinion of others.

Author and podcaster, Mel Robbins, is a good example of someone who understands the power of accepting not being accepted. In her book, *The Let Them Theory*, she shares her 'let them theory' – a mindset to help people stop worrying about the *why* and reclaim their peace. In her own words: 'If someone doesn't invite you, if someone doesn't include you, if someone doesn't value you... let them. Don't chase, don't try to convince, don't twist yourself into knots trying to be chosen. Just let them.' Sometimes people won't like you for reasons heavily out of your control – and when this happens, let them.

Closing Thoughts

Having the courage to be disliked isn't about intentionally causing drama or ruffling feathers for the sake of it. It's about having the courage to be yourself and stand by what you believe in – instead of changing or shrinking yourself to make other people feel comfortable.

You're not living softly when you are constantly performing or people-pleasing for the sake of validation and acceptance. The more you grow to understand who you are, and love yourself for being you, the more you accept that you cannot please everybody. And in accepting this, you will finally start living in true freedom – a life that isn't bound by the opinions and desires of others.

Self-reflection prompts

Which boundaries are currently working in your life?

When was the last time you said 'no' to somebody?

Is there something you want that you're too scared to ask for?

Have you ever asked for higher pay? How did that go? If you have never asked, why not?

Have you ever faced backlash for asserting a want or boundary?

Are there any areas of your life where you need to be more vocal?

How has asserting a want or boundary helped you in life?

How do you feel about being disliked by people?

What steps will you take to live more authentically?

Soft Love: Choose A Love That Nurtures You

Many people wrongly believe that possessing self-love automatically removes the desire for romantic love. This simply isn't true. While self-love is the foundation that enables you to advocate for yourself, make more informed choices, set better boundaries and define your worth beyond desiring external validation, romantic love feeds our innate desire for human connection.

Human beings are wired for emotional intimacy and companionship, and it's nothing to be embarrassed about. And while companionship can come in many forms (such as with friends and family), plenty of us still desire the type of emotional and physical intimacy we don't get from platonic relationships. Many of us want to find love, and that's perfectly normal. The hardest part of wanting companionship is finding it, and then determining whether or not it's worth keeping.

The Current Landscape

Before I delve into loving softly, I first want to discuss the current dating and relationship landscape and how, to many people, it feels far from soft. Dating has changed significantly since the time of our parents and grandparents. One obvious and unavoidable change is the way in which technology has altered how we meet and choose partners.

Historically, meeting a potential suitor required making the effort to leave the house and socialise in person. Or, if you weren't meeting people while casually or formally out and about, perhaps you'd meet them at work, or be introduced to them by a friend. Put simply, dating pre-social media was very much about meeting people via real life social networks, not digital ones.

Fast-forward to the current day; according to popular wedding planning website The Knot, most couples nowadays meet online. The website surveyed nearly 8,000 recently engaged couples in 2024, and found that 30 per cent of them met on an app – which represented the most common way people had met. This may not seem too odd initially, but when you consider statistics suggesting that less than 2 per cent of people met their partners online in the nineties, it reflects a massive change in our approach to dating.

Just thirty years ago, over a third of people met their partner through friends, and work or school was the next most common way, followed by via family, or at parties and similar gatherings. In the nineties, finding love over the web was the least common way to meet someone, and now, it's the most common. But what does that mean for dating? Is this a good or bad thing? I guess we could argue that dating apps have made it easier to connect with people on a global scale...

Once upon a time, meeting someone who lived on the other side of the world was close to impossible unless you or they had travelled. Nowadays you can fall in love from the UK with someone who lives in Australia – having never met in person at all. However, we could also argue that while connection feels 'easier', online dating has created a bit of a paradox – making connection feel less intentional but more transactional. For some people, it's not about the journey – getting to know someone deeply and working to build a meaningful connection – but rather, what they will gain at the end, from all the online befriending and swiping.

Dating online can also create the illusion of choice. Having access to an array of options can make it very hard for someone to simply choose one. People may find themselves second-guessing, constantly asking themselves whether the grass is greener elsewhere, or even believing that every option is viable and available to them – when that really isn't the case. Additionally, the sheer choice can encourage people to search for love in a shallow way – chasing connections based on superficial traits alone (like a person's profile photo), instead of connecting in a way that explores character or real depth. When you're endlessly swiping through profile after profile, it's very easy to reduce an entire person to a first impression based solely on how aesthetically pleasing their online page is. The gamification of many online dating apps has also turned dating into a sport for many people. They optimise their page for validation, and swipe for validation, while having no real desire for a deep connection. That dopamine hit they get from being 'liked' or 'messaged' is the only thing they care for.

Where 'old school' dating may have felt exciting for our parents in many ways, online dating can quickly feel fatiguing, with each interaction lacking any real variety or emotional intimacy.

Before social media apps, dating was rooted in proximity, but now it can feel as if it's more about online vanity metrics and 'hot' photos, instead of shared values and interests.

Now, that's not to say all forms of socialising online are bad. Personally, I've found it to prove successful, having met my husband via a social media app, and I know many people who have successfully partnered and are in happy relationships following online dating. However, what I think separates the successful interactions from some of the not so successful ones, is how people choose to use online platforms.

My husband and I first encountered one another on Instagram. Unbeknownst to me, he was one of my social media followers, and regularly reshared my thoughts on his stories. One day, while scrolling through my notifications, I noticed a comment under one of my posts about dating. It was a positive comment, but the profile picture looked like it was coming from a man's page (this stood out to me because I was very used to men not interacting with my content, unless they wanted to troll me in some way).

Upon clicking on the man's profile, I was greeted with an array of photos that drew my attention. To be frank, he was the most attractive man that had ever interacted with my Instagram page. I noticed he was based in the US, but having previously been in a long-distance relationship, that didn't concern me. I was immediately intrigued by his handsome looks, but with that said, I'm not one to go for style over substance, so I scrolled through his content to get a better idea of what he was about. His content was varied – some funny, some intellectual, some light-hearted and some meaningful. I remember coming across one specific video where he talked about a date he had gone on in the past and mentioned that the woman was pleasantly surprised that he didn't try to sleep with her afterwards. He proceeded to break down how terrible the dating market is – and how the poor behaviour of many men has lowered the bar so much that some women end up viewing the bare minimum as impressive, and praise basic human decency as if it's something special. After I saw that video, I followed him back.

We slowly started interacting with one another (to be fair he had been interacting with me for years, but I just hadn't noticed). Friendly replies and innocent comments continued for two months, until he eventually asked me for my number to 'get to know who I am outside of social media'. I gave him my number, and he called me two hours and ten minutes later. Our 'introductory call' was just over two hours long, and the next day he called me again. Our second call was seven hours and seventeen minutes long. We proceeded to talk every day on the phone, and two weeks later, he had already bought a ticket to visit me in the UK. Within four weeks he arrived, and by this point we had already established that we were 'official'. We spent the week of Valentine's 2022 together, and it was one of the most beautiful weeks of my life. From that point, it was us.

I believe that social media proved successful for my husband and me because of how we chose to use it. To start with, when I followed my husband, I did so based on a deep dive into his page with a focus on character over appearance. Sure, his handsome face drew me in, but it was the messaging behind his content that sealed the deal for me. Similarly, when I ask my husband about why he followed me, his reply has always been 'I just loved your mind. Your looks were a plus, but it was your mind that did it for me.'

We were intentional with our selection process, *and* with our communication. My husband could have continued our discussions over Instagram, keeping things light-hearted and surface level, but instead he asked for my number, and made it clear he wanted to explore my personality outside of social media. Moving our conversations off the app to a phone, meant we could have lengthier discussions and explore our connection in more detail, and in a more emotive way – incorporating seeing one another via FaceTime, assessing body language and considering tone. When we started speaking on the phone, we reclaimed our conversation and connection with a shared purpose in mind.

With this said, I'm aware that it doesn't matter how intentional you are willing to be if your intent and effort isn't reciprocated. As far as many women are concerned (including myself), misogyny is on the rise – making dating even harder. Worryingly, hatred for women seems louder than ever, thanks to the rise of 'manosphere red-pill' content.

According to the Oxford Dictionary, the 'manosphere' refers to 'websites and blogs where men express opinions about issues concerning contemporary masculinity and male relationships with women, especially those associated with views that are hostile to feminism and women's rights', with red-pill content referring to content that dramatically transforms men's views in a dangerous and disturbing way. This has subsequently given rise to the use of the term 'incel' – meaning involuntarily celibate.

The term was originally coined in 1997 by a woman named Alana and was used as part of an empathetic project titled 'Alana's Involuntary Celibacy Project'. Alana created a website for people who were struggling to find love and described the website in a BBC interview as a 'friendly place' where men and women could open up to one another about feeling lonely. During that time, the term incel was used mutually by both men and women and was expressed compassionately to define a person who experienced bouts of isolation and low confidence. Many years later, the term was co-opted by male-dominated groups who turned a term used to express vulnerability to one used to express misogyny and resentment towards women – blaming them for their loneliness and lack of dating success.

Over time, 'incel culture' evolved into a darker subculture, with a selection of men promoting emotional and/or physical violence against women and girls. Because of the way it has been co-opted, as it stands today, incel culture is used to describe a rebellion against women and feminism, and hasn't only shaped how some men see women, but also how women see men. In many ways, it's fractured trust between women and men.

The rise of misogynistic content has women feeling undervalued, disrespected and unsafe. One quick scroll through the likes of X (formerly Twitter) or TikTok is sadly all it takes to find messaging from men demeaning women or manipulating women to get what they want. Social media also has a tendency towards amplifying the most extreme voices, which means that people are often exposed to the most heinous and violent opinions from hateful men. Then some men choose extremism in an attempt to simply be noticed, which further feeds distrust and disgust in women. Even more concerning, is the rise of real-world attacks against women that have been linked to men who follow incel ideology. In fact, the violent attacks are so widely heard, seen and felt that the impact of incel ideology has even found its way into popular media, with shows like the 2025 Netflix psychological crime drama, *Adolescence*, detailing how red-pill content is affecting young boys, and by extension young girls.

Now, what do you think has happened to women's perspectives in the face of this hate, violence and dangerous content? The rise of this kind of content has deeply affected how many women see men. Countless women are simply fed up and they're no longer afraid to say so. Their frustration and distrust has become louder and more visible. This collective distrust has helped fuel what's often described as an ongoing 'gender war', with women expressing exhaustion at feeling unprotected or unloved by men, and men feeling personally attacked by generalisations about male behaviour. The result is an online environment filled with men-versus-women discourse – an endless stream of blame, defensiveness and misunderstanding. It's an echo chamber that has contributed to dating becoming harder for everyone, especially for those who struggle to separate fact from fear, emotion from evidence, or isolated experiences from universal truths.

But in and amongst these expressions of hate, violence and distrust, are people who continue to enjoy their dating journeys. While they do not disregard vital information regarding the current situation, they also do not absorb everything they see and hear online wholesale. They filter out what is helpful and what is unhelpful, by considering multiple things. One of which is the source behind the message – 'Who is speaking, and do I want that person's results?' They also consider the intent behind the message – 'Was this message fuelled by bitterness and created in an attempt to incite hatred or is this a carefully curated message aimed at helping me make better decisions?' Lastly, they consider the accuracy of the message – 'Are these generalisations based on anecdotal evidence or is there factual statistic evidence to support this information?'

In my opinion, people are more likely to report positive experiences whilst dating, when they know how to drown out the noise and make sound judgements based not on viral videos filled with misinformation or oversimplifications but on personal experiences, priorities and desires. While they may not disregard everything they see, they do a decent job of not letting everything they see control how they negotiate the real world.

This is one massive part of loving softly – loving in a way that centres your own feelings. Loving in a way that is grounded in personal awareness. When you don't love softly, you seek external validation and direction in all your choices. This will mean that your choices are rarely yours – but someone else's, because the decisions you make aren't initiated with you in mind but rather, how friends or family may perceive you, what strangers will think, or whether they align with the general online consensus. People who love softly, choose their lovers based on their own assessments and they don't let online noise harden their hearts in a way that encourages them to approach dating with anger or suspicion. Instead, they form their own opinions through real experiences and personal discernment.

Soft Love Isn't Fearful

Many people are scared of love. After all, loving somebody is one of the biggest risks we can take. There's always the chance it won't go how we pictured, and when that occurs, we can find ourselves grappling with feelings of anger, sadness, shame, regret, loneliness or even unrequited love. Loving isn't without risk, but with that said, our fears shouldn't control us.

After the relationship between me and my now husband became public knowledge, I was inundated with a range of projections from people regarding the 'risk' I was undertaking. They ranged from acquaintances and strangers letting me know they would never enter a long-distance relationship down to their partner having too much 'freedom' and them possessing a lack of trust, to people asking me how I would feel should the relationship not work out after being 'social media official', to strangers stating they would never share photos of themselves and their partner online unless they were married. Much of the discourse surrounded the risk of potential embarrassment at the hands of a partner.

Interestingly, the projections I encountered regarding people's anxiety about visibility, trust and the risk of public failure, highlighted a wider social undercurrent that was brought to my attention later on in 2025. *British Vogue* published an article by writer Chanté Joseph that went viral, titled 'Is Having a Boyfriend Embarrassing Now?'

The piece highlighted how in recent years, for many heterosexual women, having a boyfriend or publicly showcasing that relationship has become culturally less appealing and thus 'embarrassing'. Joseph explored the potential reasons for this, including a move away from women defining themselves by their partnership status (i.e., being in a relationship isn't the 'achievement' it once was), and how being seen in a conventional relationship online can feel performative or limiting in a time where female independence is prized.

The virality of the article highlighted how many women today hesitate to share their relationships publicly, not because they're necessarily ashamed of love, but because being perceived as being tied to a man has somehow become a bit of a cultural faux pas (largely down to the social failings of men in general).

I personally adore how women are evolving, and I understand why that article was so widely shared and loved. I actually agree that for the most part, men are embarrassing. But I would also argue that love in and of itself can feel very embarrassing.

When we choose to love someone, we expose them to the most vulnerable parts of who we are. We admit a desire for companionship, and in admitting we care deeply for someone, we open ourselves up to the possibility of hurt. Love is a risk because it requires stepping into uncertainty with no guarantees of how the relationship will develop. In loving anyone, you offer them access to the softest parts of you, knowing that there is always a risk they could end up hurting you in a multitude of ways. On social media, that feeling is amplified.

When you share your relationship with the world, people project, comment and compare. In sharing your love publicly, you invite an audience into something intimate, and if that love should not stand the test of time, the opinions of others and the comments on your 'failure' can certainly make you feel ashamed or embarrassed. I say all this to acknowledge that 'embarrassment' is part of the process – whether your relationship is public knowledge or not. You can't choose love without risking embarrassment, and in loving openly, you will always be viewed as embarrassing in the eyes of someone.

The irony for me now, is that I am in a happy and loving marriage that would never have existed had I given in to people's projections, or possessed the fear of embarrassment myself. Instead, I chose to love freely. Don't get me wrong – I still applied discernment, but I did so with an absence of fear.

I want to encourage you to do the same. Love freely but wisely. What did that look like for me? Instead of being distrusting about every display of affection, I paid most attention to **what was done**, over *what was promised*. I learned to value **actions** over words. And when it did come down to words, I listened with **awareness** and *not suspicion*. I didn't rush to assume the worst but rather, I **heard with the aim of understanding the other person** over *'catching them out'*. And on the occasion that I didn't understand, I would **ask questions to better understand and connect**, rather than *pull away* or *stonewall*.

I know some people reading this may be thinking, 'you've probably never been hurt before', but that's far from the truth. I have written an entire book dedicated to retelling some of my personal heartbreaks and what I did to recover from them. I've been undervalued, cheated on and much more, but I still didn't allow those negative experiences to limit my capacity to love.

The thing about past trauma is that while we may not have caused it, it's our responsibility to work on healing ourselves – with the understanding that healing is a continuous journey and the goal at the end is not perfection, but rather a willingness to keep going without living in fear of how our past will show up in our present or future.

Soft love is willing, and soft lovers choose to love in a way that de-centres fear. They are not controlled by their past, but rather, they use their past to help them make decisions that inform them instead of control them. Soft lovers love from a place of connection before protection. This doesn't mean they don't protect themselves – they still establish boundaries and remain strict about them, but they approach relationships with the thought that people are innocent *unless* proven guilty – instead of guilty until proven innocent. When you choose to embark on your relationships assuming immediate guilt, you ultimately approach them in a guarded way that is devoid of vulnerability, which only limits your opportunity for connection and growth.

Instead of being controlled by fears, be guided by hope. Hope about your outcomes, the love stories you have yet to experience, the people you have yet to encounter, the meaningful memories that lie ahead. Hope is not naive. It's courageous, freeing, and the most powerful example of vulnerability.

Soft Love Is Intentional

An important part of feeling more at ease when you are dating, is dating with intentionality – particularly when it comes to what you are looking for in a partner. While selecting with intent does not mean you are at zero-risk of heartbreak, it certainly reduces the risk, as you're focusing on what truly matters, not just what feels good in the moment. And while every relationship is different, and we all look for different things, I do think that there are some underlying features and characteristics that we should all look out for in a potential partner.

Respect

In romantic relationships, people often want to feel desired and admired, but to be respected is to be truly loved. When a person respects you, they recognise that your value is inherent and doesn't need to be proven to them. When a person respects you, they speak to you kindly – even during moments of anger or sadness. When you're respected, your thoughts and beliefs are not dismissed, and your boundaries are honoured. Your vulnerabilities and weaknesses are also not used against you. When someone respects you, they view you as a whole person who is experiencing their own life, and they don't seek to diminish or control you. A love story without respect, can never be love.

Honesty

While every relationship is unique, and each person has their own boundaries and non-negotiables, one quality that consistently reflects a wholesome connection is honesty. Even in mutually non-monogamous relationships, honesty remains essential as it allows people to communicate transparently and build trust through clarity and not secrecy. In a healthy relationship, honesty isn't just about confessing mistakes or sharing facts – it's about creating safety to share the truth. And when honesty is present, there's no need for guessing games and no feelings of constant anxiety or worry. Where honesty exists, you know your love isn't based on illusion or façade but rather, truth-telling and open-ended, trustworthy communication.

Understanding

Understanding is the bridge between honesty and feeling heard. In a healthy relationship, understanding shows up when you and your partner try to hear what the other one truly means, not simply listening to respond. When we seek to understand someone, we create room for grace, consideration and patience. We also ask questions for clarity, and we dig deeper to build closeness. Two people in a relationship who understand each other, see each other in ways strangers can't, picking up on context clues, body language and so much more. When understanding exists in a relationship, people don't walk on eggshells because both parties are free to express themselves with vulnerability. When you are understood, you feel truly seen.

Self-awareness

A good partner is also a self-aware one. Self-awareness determines how a person recognises their own emotions, personal flaws, triggers and weaknesses. A self-aware person is reflective, and being able to reflect is one way we not only take accountability, but we also limit ourselves from projecting our frustrations onto our partner. The ability to be self-aware also makes a person more respectful, as they are better at processing their emotions and therefore more likely to pause and think during conflict, instead of reacting in anger. Self-awareness contributes to growth in a relationship, and brings about softness by improving understanding and limiting reactionary and defensive behaviour.

Supportiveness

A supportive partner wants to see you evolve and will demonstrate this by verbally encouraging you and/or physically helping you to reach your goals – even when the benefits of you succeeding don't directly impact them. When a relationship lacks support, that creates room for competition and resentment. It can also encourage one party to shrink or dull themselves in an attempt to not 'ruffle feathers' in a way that intimidates their partner. A soft love is expansive, and that can only occur where mutual support exists. In a healthy relationship, your evolution should be supported, and you should each be able to grow without fear of outgrowing one another.

Shared Values

When people mention 'values', they're usually referring to the principles and beliefs people align with that determine how they choose to live. Values shape our moral compass and priorities – what we see as right and wrong, or important and unimportant. For example, things like respect, honesty, faith and family are all values. When you don't share values with a person, you're more likely to clash on issues that you view as non-negotiable or significant to you. Prioritising shared values in a relationship places you and your partner on the 'same page' – creating more space for harmony and moving in the same direction, especially on important issues.

Closing Thoughts

Soft love isn't about pretending that the dating landscape is peaceful – it's OK to acknowledge the challenges. Loving softly is about choosing peace for yourself. In a time where dating can feel transactional, suspicious or 'embarrassing', choosing to love with open-hearted vulnerability can almost feel radical.

Soft love is about remaining hopeful and open even when you may have heard or seen reasons to be fearful and closed off. To love softly is to love intentionally – learn what you value, what you need, and remain strict about it. Modern dating may not always reward loving gently, but showing up as the most open and vulnerable version of yourself will encourage alignment by attracting people who are willing to be and accept the same in return.

Self-reflection prompts

What are you most fearful of when it comes to love?

How does that fear impact the way you navigate relationships?

What does loving vulnerably look like to you?

Beyond the qualities listed in this chapter, what other qualities do you want your future partner to have?

Who taught you what love should look like, and how much of that still aligns with who you are today?

When you picture a partner who brings you peace, what qualities stand out beyond physical attraction and financial status?

Soft Health: Honour What Your Body Tells You

In a world that glorifies constantly being on the go and hustling hard, many of us have forgotten how to slow down and listen to our body. We push through so much – stress, exhaustion and tension – often ignoring the signs that we need to take a pause. While our bodies are powerful vessels, they are also sensitive and need to be treated with the utmost care. Living softly requires you to listen to your body.

The Impact of Stress

'I can't come and kill myself.' If you're unfamiliar with this phrase, it may seem extreme – but if you *are* familiar with it, you probably chuckled or nodded in agreement. It's a Nigerian Pidgin English saying, which was popularised further by international music artist Burna Boy, who included it in his hit song 'Ye'. It's a phrase that emphasises the importance of self-care and not stressing over things that are largely out of your control. To define it further, 'I can't come and kill myself' simply means 'I refuse to over-exert myself or stress myself out to the point that it messes with my health and wellbeing.' This Nigerian phrase is one that I personally live by, and I probably repeat it about twice a week.

I'm a big believer in doing whatever you can to minimise stress in your life – whether it's through saying 'no' to things that don't serve you, learning to simply 'let things go', resting, or opting for convenience and working 'smart' over working 'hard'. Stress and I are sworn enemies, and I do what I can to be as far away from stress as possible.

One thing I've been vocal about in previous books and interviews, is how seriously stress can impact my body. A physical marker of stress on me that I've discussed openly in the past is vitiligo. For those who are unaware, vitiligo is a skin condition characterised by a loss of melanin, causing a person's skin to turn 'white' in certain areas. Many present and past public figures have spoken openly about having vitiligo, such as the likes of Canadian model Winnie Harlow (who has used her fame to advocate for the inclusion and acceptance of people with the condition), Michael Jackson, the 'King of Pop' (who spoke in interviews about his changing complexion and cited vitiligo as the cause), and actor Jon Hamm (who suggested his own vitiligo was caused by stress while filming *Mad Men*). Like Hamm, my vitiligo was stress-induced, appearing in two stages during two separate stressful events in my life – initially as a child and then again in my twenties.

Moving from Nigeria to the UK was a significant change for me to process as a child. Moving from a predominantly Black country with certain customs and behaviours I had grown used to, to being in a predominantly white country, city and school proved challenging for me at times. In addition, the geographical change contributed to adjustments in my home life that also proved challenging for my parents, and that stress rubbed off on me. This is when my vitiligo first appeared, spreading again in my early twenties following the toxic relationship I was in while at university. I know first-hand how impactful stress can be on the body – based solely on what I could physically see on myself.

Stress in Women

Here's a not so fun fact for you... According to the American Psychological Association, chronic stress is most prevalent among women. Unfortunately, I can't say I was particularly surprised by this fact when I first heard it. Having seen how stress has manifested in my personal life, as well as in the lives of women I know, I understand how and why this is true. It's no secret that the average woman faces certain social and structural challenges the average man doesn't have to navigate – whether it's having a job while simultaneously managing a household and caring for loved ones, taking on the mental labour of maintaining social relationships and fulfilling other people's emotional needs, or navigating the gender pay gap, gender discrimination and glass ceilings. It's a lot. Not to forget, simply existing in a world where there is an epidemic of violence against women and girls... When you couple all of this with hormonal changes like menstruation, pregnancy, perimenopause and menopause, it's no surprise that the world is a stressful place for many women. Sadly, that stress is harming us in ways we may not even realise. Numerous large-scale surveys have consistently shown that women report not only higher rates of stress but also more severe chronic stress than men. We are also more likely to report feeling overwhelmed and emotionally exhausted, as well as higher rates of stress-related disorders like anxiety and depression.

One 2018 JAMA (*Journal of the American Medical Association*) study that examined over 100,000 individuals diagnosed with stress-related disorders (such as PTSD and acute stress), found that 'stressed' individuals had a 30–40 per cent increased risk of developing autoimmune disease (including lupus, rheumatoid arthritis, Crohn's and multiple sclerosis), when compared with both their siblings and the general population. The ten-year study titled 'Association of Stress-Related Disorders with Subsequent

Autoimmune Disease', by Huan Song and colleagues, determined a strong link between psychological stress/trauma and the onset of autoimmune diseases – reinforcing the biological link between chronic stress, body inflammation and immunity issues. Unsurprisingly, when compared with men, women had significantly higher rates of autoimmune disease – which logically makes sense, considering that chronic stress is most prevalent among women.

This unfortunate reality was further highlighted in a 2024 scientific review by professor of medicine and immunology, DeLisa Fairweather, titled 'Mechanisms underlying sex differences in autoimmunity'. The review noted that 'most autoimmune diseases occur more often in women than men'. According to the study, women are eight times more likely than men to be diagnosed with lupus – a chronic autoimmune disease, which leads to the immune system mistakenly attacking healthy tissue and organs, causing inflammation and pain throughout the body. The review also highlighted that women are twice as likely as men to be diagnosed with rheumatoid arthritis – a chronic autoimmune disease that occurs when the immune system mistakenly attacks the lining of the joints, causing stiffness and pain in them.

The evidence is clear: when the body is placed under prolonged stress, it doesn't simply affect the mind – it leaves physical traces too. Chronic stress can dysregulate the immune system, heighten inflammation and make us more vulnerable to long-term illness. Over time, what starts as emotional strain can quite literally manifest as disease in the body.

Hard Choices for Soft Living

The truth of the matter is that in order for women to live softly and combat our higher risk of autoimmune disease, we must prioritise our health by forming healthy habits.

Admittedly, if there's one area of soft living that I struggle with the most, it's making healthy and productive lifestyle choices regarding what I consume and how I choose to spend my free time. I'm great at some things – like being kind to myself, not people-pleasing, managing stress, resting and balancing my career – but the thing that always feels a little tougher to me is diet, exercise and making the 'healthier choice'.

One important aspect of soft living that I cannot ignore is what our bodies consume – beyond media and entertainment. What am I talking about? I'm talking about the links between processed foods, alcohol consumption, lack of exercise, exposure to chemicals and chronic illness. Just review what the average diet looks like in places like the US or UK.

Much of our food is ultra-processed and chemically reformulated – with a focus on preservation rather than providing nourishment. Something as common as your everyday supermarket loaf of bread can be full of preservatives or made with refined flour stripped of fibre and micronutrients. Your favourite morning cereal may be made from refined grains and full of flavourings. That convenient jar of pasta sauce you love so much? Sugar, preservatives, refined oils, and a whole lot of other stuff you may not even be able to accurately pronounce. Then there are the instant meals, the sodas, the snacks, the processed meats, the frozen pizzas... Don't get me wrong, I have consumed a bunch of this stuff (and still do), so I'm not sharing this to lambast you in any way. But the reality of the world we live in is that a lot of us are consuming crap, and it's making us worse off.

There's an abundant amount of research confirming how the consumption of ultra-processed foods correlates with an increased risk of diabetes, heart disease, obesity, and even depression. Unhealthy foods don't just impact how our bodies look on the outside. They disrupt the way our bodies regulate themselves – contributing to fatigue, low mood or sickness.

Then there's alcohol. I'm personally not a big drinker, and throughout university (when people typically experience their most intense periods of drinking) I was teetotal, meaning I didn't drink at all. I didn't start consuming alcohol until I was 24, and since then I've enjoyed the occasional sweet cocktail on a night out, or the odd shot when my cousins are in town, but for the most part, I don't drink much when compared with the average person in the UK. And as far as my health is concerned, not drinking much has been an easy win for me.

Despite alcohol being completely legal and marketed as a recreational drink for relaxation and enjoyment, it kills more people per year than cocaine and cannabis, according to the World Health Organization (WHO). In fact, death aside, in 2023 the WHO shared that 'no level of alcohol consumption is safe for our health'. As accessible as it might be, alcohol is classified as a Group 1 carcinogen (the highest risk group) by the International Agency for Research on Cancer – alongside things like asbestos and even radiation.

We now know that even moderate consumption of alcohol is associated with increased risks of a range of diseases, and not just cancer. The World Heart Federation confirms an increased risk of heart disease in alcohol drinkers, while liver disease continues to be the most common alcohol-caused disease. A 2008 study titled 'The relationship between alcohol consumption and cortisol secretion in an aging cohort' by E. Badrick and colleagues, also highlights the way alcohol amplifies hormones like the stress hormone cortisol, often making drinkers feel worse off in the long run.

I know that outside of having a taste for it, many people reach for a drink to ease social anxiety and find confidence in moments that may feel a little awkward or uncomfortable. While that might seem harmless, it teaches you to associate socialising with the relief that alcohol provides, and with time, your body (and mind) slowly become reliant on alcohol to boost dopamine and suppress your cortisol levels. The problem with this is how will you ever learn to find confidence or soothe your social anxiety when you always use alcohol as a buffer?

Numbing your discomfort is far from living softly. Instead, regulate your emotions before entering social spaces – whether that's through breathing exercises, power posing or even bringing a companion along. When your nervous system feels at peace, you're less likely to feel as if you need a drink. Reframing what confidence looks like is also helpful. You don't have to be the loudest in the room, the centre of attention or the most vigorous dancer. Simply showing up, listening and engaging with others displays a lot of confidence. You don't have to impress to connect, you just have to be yourself.

The True Cost of Beauty

Beyond what we eat and drink, there are other types of consumption that can have a significant impact on the body. It's what we apply to our skin, what our bodies absorb, and all the things we inhale – from our favourite scented candles to cleaning sprays.

Whether it's skincare, make-up or general household items, the truth stands that many contain something called EDCs (endocrine-disrupting chemicals). EDCs are chemicals that can interfere with the body's endocrine system – the system in charge of creating and releasing hormones to regulate things like our reproduction, mood, growth, metabolism, and how our bodies operate in general.

According to the National Institute of Environmental Health Sciences, when this system is interfered with, EDCs work at mimicking or altering our hormones, which can lead to a range of health issues like certain cancers, reproductive health issues and developmental problems. In fact, you may already be aware of the names of certain EDCs without even realising it.

Have you ever purchased a bottle of shampoo and read 'paraben free'? Parabens are a group of preservatives commonly used in beauty products like conditioners and shampoos. Their purpose? They help to prevent the growth of things like mould and bacteria, but in 2018 researchers at George Mason University in Virginia found that women who used cosmetic products with higher paraben concentrations had abnormal reproductive hormone levels. The study, by Professor of Global and Community Health, Dr Anna Pollack, confirmed early indicators that chemicals such as parabens may increase oestrogen levels, with high levels potentially affecting reproductive health.

The same is true for BPA, short for Bisphenol A. When I hear or see 'BPA' I immediately think of one thing – plastic bottles. Or at least, that's how I came to know about it. BPA is a synthetic chemical used to make things like plastic, but its bad reputation comes from the fact that it can cause hormonal imbalances – leading to a range of health concerns and issues, including reproductive, developmental and cardiovascular problems.

A 2019 *Current Molecular Pharmacology* research paper links BPA exposure (even at low levels) with an increased risk of hormone-related cancers, such as breast cancer, ovarian cancer and prostate cancer. The study by Shirin A. Hafezi & Wael M. Abdel-Rahman emphasised the need for regulation of exposure, and factoring in BPA effects in cancer-prevention strategies. Yet the likes of parabens, BPA, and so much more can be found in a vast number of everyday products – so what can we do to protect ourselves?

To start, please read labels. I read labels for lots of things – from the shampoo I use, to the food I purchase. There is even a range of apps you can download on your phone that essentially read labels for you, highlighting problematic ingredients. And don't assume that if something appears healthy, it automatically is.

I once went grocery shopping in the US with my husband who was my boyfriend at the time. I purchased some smoked salmon, which is technically processed (any food that has been altered from its natural state is processed), but it's on the healthier end of the 'processed spectrum'. Now in my mind, I had assumed the salmon was processed in a way that simply involved curing and smoking. Imagine my surprise when I got home to open the packaging, only for my hands to be stained with what appeared to be orange highlighter. I subsequently read the back of the fish packet and discovered that it had been artificially coloured. I was aghast.

In light of everything I've shared, I don't want you thinking I'm a perfect person when it comes to limiting my exposure to toxic chemicals. I still have the odd drink and stuff my face with processed junk food on occasion, and even worse, for some years I slapped chemical relaxer on my head when I was sporting a pixie cut. I'm no angel in the diet and chemical exposure department. However, the one thing I will stress is that's it's important to know what's going in or on your body so you can make informed decisions and adjustments where you see fit. In using lots of one ingredient, you might minimise your use of another, or maybe you choose to go as natural as you can.

Sleep is Non-Negotiable

'Please sleep more... For me.' This is a sentence I uttered more than once when I started dating my husband. Why? The man just wouldn't sleep. OK, not literally. He'd sleep, but for only a few hours. And when the recommended amount of sleep for an adult is 7–9 hours, a few hours just won't cut it.

Part of the reason I would almost beg him to sleep, is because I understood the toll that lack of sleep has on the body. In fact, I've experienced it first-hand. Sleep is one of those things my body simply can't scrimp on, largely because the impact that not sleeping has on my body is hellish. With less than six hours' sleep across two days or more, I fall victim to debilitating migraines, low mood and breakouts. It's a big reason why one thing I really don't play with, is my sleep. In fact, when my family met my husband while we were dating, they warned him to never get in between me and my sleep. Really! They were 100 per cent correct, because the worst version of me exists on low sleep. I'm moody, I'm irritable and I'm uninterested in anything but topping my sleep up.

While the effects of poor sleep may not be so obvious on everyone's body, the fact is, it negatively impacts everyone, whether they know it or not. In fact, many neuroscientists agree that sleep is the most important thing human beings need for good health. One of these neuroscientists is Matthew Walker, director of the Center for Human Sleep Science at UC Berkeley and author of *Why We Sleep*. In the words of Walker, 'sleep is the single most effective thing we can do to reset our mental and physical health each day'. In his book, Walker states that there is a direct relationship between how well we sleep and how long we live, and almost nobody can get away with fewer than six hours of sleep a night without harming their health.

Sleep is the foundation for how our body operates. While diet and exercise are important, adequate sleep is needed for exercise recovery, and no amount of good dieting can override chronic sleep debt.

When you assess how poor sleep can impact the body, it is truly terrifying. In his book, Walker states that the physical and cognitive health effects of sleeping poorly include impaired memory and focus, an increased risk of stroke and heart attack, an increased risk of diabetes, a higher chance of experiencing anxiety and depression, faster ageing, immune disorders and so much more.

> 'I'll sleep when I'm dead' is hustle culture's favourite quote, but the twisted irony is you'll certainly die if you don't sleep. When you play with your sleep, you play with your health and your life.

If you're reading this as someone who doesn't value sleep enough, I hate to break it to you but you're not living softly. You're building a foundation for a very hard future filled with ailments, rapid ageing and a slow, dull mind. And if you're reading this as a woman who doesn't value sleep, you're at even greater risk of issues. There are several surveys and studies suggesting women generally need more sleep than men. Hormonal fluctuations and differing social demands, coupled with differences in our circadian rhythm (our body's internal 24-hour clock), contribute to why our body (and brains) require more downtime.

If you want to save your health while you can, there *are* some things you can do to facilitate sleep prioritisation and sleeping well.

Optimise your sleep environment

Three things that really mess with my sleep are polyester sheets, hot rooms and too much light. When I mention polyester sheets, I'm not even trying to be bougie. Simply put, synthetic materials aren't 'breathable', so they trap heat and often make people feel clammy and uncomfortable. I don't need a nine-hundred-thread-count bedsheet or duvet cover to sleep comfortably, but I, like many other people, am much better off sleeping in natural fibres. Cotton, linen, bamboo or eucalyptus sheets are breathable and also work alongside your body's natural cooling process.

Temperature is such an important factor for sleeping well. Studies have found that people experience improved sleep when they sleep in a room that is slightly cooler than room temperature (ideally 18 degrees Celsius/65 degrees Fahrenheit). Anything significantly colder or warmer can cause restlessness, as your body is working overtime to restore a sense of balance. When it's too hot or too cold, your heart rate fluctuates, and your cortisol levels are raised – so your body will struggle to fall into a deep state of sleep. And while you may sleep for hours in a cold or hot environment, you will often find yourself waking up feeling unrested.

Too much light also has a similar effect on the body, keeping it alert when it should be resting. I remember visiting a close friend in my twenties and staying over at her place on more than one occasion. While I loved her company, I absolutely hated sleeping in her bedroom. Have you ever slept in a room with Venetian blinds or thin curtains? My friend had very thin curtains at the time, and the second the sun rose, the room would be filled with light. Sounds beautiful when you say it out loud, doesn't it? It wasn't. It was painful. Even after a night on the town that saw us getting in at 2 a.m., I would rise at 6 a.m. – with the sun. Bear in mind, this wasn't willingly! I just couldn't sleep through all the light. To this day, the same rings true.

Beyond my mild irritation (justified!), there is actual evidence to back me up here. Too much light during sleep suppresses melatonin (a natural hormone your body produces to regulate the sleep cycle).

When you don't have enough melatonin in your body, you can experience insomnia, drowsiness during the daytime and low mood. Melatonin is such a powerful hormone in sleep, that Global Market Insights suggest the US melatonin supplements market was valued at about $2.84 billion in 2024. In fact, melatonin is so powerful that in the UK it's classed as a prescription-only medicine and cannot be found on store shelves. Your body needs melatonin to sleep well, and you need to sleep well to live healthily.

Protect Your Health

Another part of healthy living is protecting your health on a regular basis. I could sit here and tell you how important it is to exercise, but let's be honest – you already know this. It's not breaking news that regular exercise keeps your heart strong, strengthens your bones and muscles, supports your brain, regulates your mood and fortifies your immune system. Countless research has proven that people who engage in weekly exercise have a higher life expectancy and a much lower risk of disease, depression and age-related decline. To live healthily, you have to exercise, and there's no way around it.

So, I want to talk to you about another aspect of protecting your health that is rarely discussed so openly... Let's talk about sex. If we aren't having it, we've had it, or we will have it – and it's important to understand the ways sex can impact the body. And don't worry – I'm not going to preach to you about how sex is bad and you should protect yourself by rarely/never engaging in it. The actual truth is that when done with care and mutual respect, sex can enhance your soft life. Sex can bring about a range of physical and emotional benefits, including lowering cortisol levels, supporting cardiovascular health, improving sleep, reducing stress and even enhancing personal confidence. Good sex is good for the body, but bad sex can be life changing – and not in a positive way.

> To live softly, you must first believe that your body is worth protecting, and that includes not being careless about sex.

It's astonishing to me how casual neglect of sexual health is sometimes pushed as a form of liberation... It simply isn't. While casual sex can be enjoyable and shouldn't automatically be stigmatised, being careless about your sexual health during casual or non-casual encounters just makes you vulnerable, and highlights a disregard you have for your body, as well as the disregard you have for your partner's body. In protecting yourself, you also protect other people you are intimate with, and the wider impact of good sexual health habits is important for every community. Unprotected sex can expose you and your partner to a range of infections and health risks. To reduce risk, use barrier methods such as condoms or dental dams, especially when trust or exclusivity hasn't been clearly established.

In 2024, the World Health Organization (WHO) warned that sexually transmitted diseases and infections are generally on the rise, and the list of diseases people might expose themselves to when they don't use protection is vast. According to the WHO, global HIV, viral hepatitis epidemics and sexually transmitted infections continue to pose significant public health challenges, causing 2.5 million deaths each year.

Some diseases and infections can remain with you for life, some can be asymptomatic – meaning you may not realise you have them – some can hinder your fertility if left untreated, and some can be resistant to antibiotics, making them significantly harder to treat. I share this not to scare you, but to say softness thrives where safety exists, and it's softer to live intentionally than recklessly – particularly when it comes to sex.

And while barrier methods aren't 100 per cent effective against all diseases and infections, they're still the most effective way to protect yourself. Through using sexual protection, regular testing, and choosing partners who value their own sexual health, you can create further safety for softness to exist.

Closing Thoughts

Living softly also means living consciously, with an understanding of what you put your body through, and what you put in it. The goal isn't to restrict yourself from every pleasure or to chase perfection – it's about minimising the physical stresses your body encounters in whichever way is comfortable for you. Each time you choose to eat cleaner, exercise more and sleep better, you are pouring into yourself, and that's the truest form of softness there is.

Self-reflection prompts

Are you happy with your current lifestyle choices? If not, why not?

How does your body usually respond to stress?

If you could let go of one food, drink or substance that doesn't serve you well any more, what would it be and why?

What small habit could you change this week to reduce stress on your body?

When was the last time you had a thorough workout?

When was the last time you got at least eight hours' sleep?

If you were to imagine your body ten years from now, what kind of care would you want to have given it?

Do you usually use barrier methods when you have sex?

How often do you get checked for sexually transmitted diseases/infections?

What choices are you making now that align with the vision of a healthier you?

Soft Work: Why Work Needs to Align with What You Value

It's estimated that the average person spends about a third of their life at work – roughly 90,000 hours, according to *Forbes*. When you take this into consideration, in my opinion, the ultimate job is one that makes all that time feel worthwhile – a job that aligns with who you are as a person and what you truly value.

A third of your life is much too long to work at a job you hate, yet many people do this. In a world that demands constant income, it's easy to feel under pressure when it comes to finding work, and as a result, many people take on jobs they dislike, purely as a matter of survival or simply because they feel 'less than' without one.

There are also people who invest in careers they dislike not because of economic pressure, but because of personal pressure. Typically, this comes from family members. As a first-generation migrant, I am very familiar with how intense this pressure can be – not because I experienced it first-hand but because I know many people who did. Despite both coming from very academic Nigerian families, my parents were rather lenient when it came to attempting to mould or drive my career choices. My mother has always been quite liberal in her world views, and my father was raised by his father, who had several degrees – including one from King's College in London, and Harvard University in the United States – two very renowned institutions. My grandfather was a traditional Nigerian disciplinarian who also happened be a high achiever, and he put a lot of pressure on my father, which he resented. This resulted in my dad being more open and understanding about my own career choices, as he didn't want to pass on that same type of generational resentment. Sadly, the same can't be said for all parents. Many apply pressure onto their children due to either experiencing that same type of pressure themselves, or feeling unaccomplished in life and subsequently attempting to live vicariously through the achievement of their kids.

When I left university, I struggled to find work, and for a while I was on Jobseeker's Allowance – a government benefit for people not in full-time employment. I remember heading to the Jobcentre every two weeks to certify I was indeed searching for work, so I could collect the assistance pay. I felt so anxious every time I would enter the building – hoping and praying nobody I knew saw me (which is silly, because if they were there, they would have been struggling to find work too – and there's no shame in struggling).

Eventually, I got a job that paid me by the hour – working in a local phone network shop, selling phones, sim cards and phone plans to people. While I didn't *hate* the job because my colleagues were nice, I felt like I wasn't earning enough, and I wasn't particularly passionate about customer service or phones for that matter. I left that job after securing a salaried role within a utility company. Now that job was one I hated! While I met some lovely people there, the customer service element was so much more painful. Selling your everyday person a phone they actually want is one thing, but managing gas and electricity for small to medium businesses was a whole different ball game. I'd often be screamed at down the phone, for things that were completely out of my control. After all, I wasn't responsible for determining energy prices. But business owners didn't care – they regularly needed someone to take their frustrations out on, and in that job, I was their punchbag.

Aside from angry customers, I had left university with a communications and media degree and felt like I was wasting money by working in a job that was completely unrelated to my former area of study. I didn't care about electricity and gas, and I hated speaking to strangers on the phone, so after two years and a *lot* of searching, I moved jobs again. This time, I landed a communications role in the NHS – the UK's national health care service. The job felt more satisfying than both of my previous jobs, largely because it was linked to my degree and it felt purposeful – I was helping clinics in my county better serve their patients, and this led to better local health outcomes.

I performed so well in my role that I was promoted to the role of regional Digital Media Manager and oversaw work that played to my strengths – like social media management and design. I even led and designed a skin cancer awareness campaign that went on to win an award. That role felt meaningful, it was aligned with my skills and I was making real change. But the two-year itch hit me again, and I left that job to take on a role at the University of Oxford as their Student Communications Manager.

This job felt prestigious, it paid better, it utilised my skills and degree, I made friends, and I felt like I was contributing something good to the student experience. Also, the job wasn't draining, which meant I had time and energy to pour into my hobbies and freelance work– like writing and social media. I would come home in the evenings after working my 9–5, to start my 5–9, which was writing online. In fact, if I'm being completely honest, sometimes I'd even do this work while I was in the office (but that's between you and me).

Over time, however, I began to grow resentful of my full-time job, because I just didn't enjoy it as much as the work I did online. My online work also felt more personal and purposeful. I would share my experiences and thoughts about dating, friendships, marriage, family and more – to be a voice to young women who were looking for guidance. So many girls and young women would get in touch with me regularly, remarking on how much my words helped them. I felt like I was making a significant difference to the lives of people who were just like me, and that meant the world to me.

Around this time, COVID hit, and many people lost their jobs while companies paused employment. I was unaffected, but that didn't prevent me from wanting to do something radical. For the first time in the role, I felt uncomfortable, and I took it as a sign that I should leave. When I raised the topic with my manager, he thought I was crazy. To him, I was working a dream – managing student communications for one of the world's top universities – and I was trying to leave during a worldwide pandemic, a time where the job landscape was turbulent and unpredictable. But in my heart, I knew it was a 'now or never' situation. So, in 2020 I took a risk, and left that job at Oxford to work for myself. Was I anxious? Of course. To a certain extent, it was a calculated risk because I had savings, still lived with my parents at the time, and knew that even if I made no money for the first few months, I could just about afford to be out of work. But on the flip side, the risk was leaving a job I liked, and walking into the unknown. 'What if I don't get another job as good as this one?' I thought. But deep down, I knew I had made the best decision for me, and I knew working for myself was the right job.

What Does the 'Right Job' Look Like?

Many of us judge careers by external standards, like how much they pay, or the prestige associated with the job title or company. In the eyes of many, money and prestige are the determiners for success, but I've met rich people who detest their job and have it purely as a means to an end. I've met people who invoke jealousy in others when they talk about what they do for a living, but day-to-day, they are stressed, underpaid and unhappy. In the words of the late writer and civil rights activist, Maya Angelou, the measure of true success is 'liking yourself, liking what you do, and liking how you do it'. This quote beautifully encompasses what the right job for you (a soft job) is all about.

When you like what you do, you remain passionate about your work. You go to work every day, not with resentment or anger but with sincere interest and enjoyment. And that passion only triggers better results, which in turn makes you prouder of the work you accomplish.

Liking what you do isn't simply about how much you get paid, but whether what you do aligns with your interests, priorities, goals, and the principles you hold dear. Liking how you work is also just as important.

I recently came across a clip of Oprah Winfrey speaking on Pastor T.D. Jakes' podcast, *NXT* Chapter. In that episode, Oprah shared what she believed was the secret behind her show being the number one show in the US for twenty-five years. She stated that in 1989 she interviewed a few Ku Klux Klan (KKK) members, thinking she was showing their vitriol to the world. However, during a commercial break she noticed them giving each other hand signals and felt uncomfortable but dismissed her feelings. Twenty years later she brought those same men back to her show, and they informed her that they had used her platform and their signals to indirectly recruit more KKK members.

That experience remained with Oprah. She learned a valuable lesson on that day; the uneasy realisation that even when your intentions are good, giving people a platform can have unintended negative consequences. This lesson was further reinforced when she invited another guest to her stage – a married man who attended the show with his wife and his mistress, to publicly admit to his wife that he was having an affair. However, during live filming things took a turn, and the man told his wife that his mistress was pregnant. Oprah remarked that everyone in the audience was so embarrassed for the man's wife and that when she saw her face, she felt her humiliation. In that moment, Oprah affirmed that such a thing would never happen again, informing her producers that she wouldn't be recording episodes like that in the future.

According to Oprah, she had read a book called *The Seat of the Soul* by Gary Zukav, which explores the idea that power comes from aligning yourself with your soul's purpose. The book argues that real fulfilment comes from inner awareness and intention, suggesting you can't have a cause and effect without having an intention behind the cause. With this newfound awareness, Oprah informed her producers that 'from this day forward we're not going to do a show until my intention is aligned with your intention. So do not bring me an idea unless you are clear about the real intention for doing it and if I can find a thread of truth in it, I can sit in the chair and be myself.'

Oprah wanted her entire team to be intentional about why they were booking guests and, in her words, 'that changed everything'. Her first Emmy eventually followed, and, on the podcast, she stressed that 'whatever project, whatever opportunity comes your way, being clear about what it is you actually really want to achieve and having everybody else in the room in alignment with that vision and how to execute that vision' is important, 'so that everybody is in synergetic vibration to bring it into fruition and manifestation'. Oprah's personal experience is a valuable reminder that even when you like what you do, you must like *how* you do it.

A fulfilling job reflects not just your values but also your intentions. What is your purpose? What are you trying to get out of it? What do you want your impact to be? If your inner intention doesn't align with the intention of the company or business, then you're in misalignment. Their mission statement and ethos should be something you believe in. And if you work for yourself, the work you do should reflect your personal values. Liking how you do things speaks to your integrity in the workplace and reflects taking pride in your choices, efforts, techniques and routine. In liking how you work, you're being true to yourself and your personal moral compass. Maintaining this integrity is also one path towards liking who you are.

We touched on self-love previously, and liking who you are is also important when it comes to your career. You could even argue that self-love is the foundation that determines the type of job you choose and how you interpret your success. Are you hard on yourself? Do you judge yourself according to comparison and societal markers? Or do you prioritise your wellbeing and focus on defining your own fulfilment?

> When you like yourself, your identity isn't dependant on accolades, salaries, external validation or senior titles, because you don't need your career to prove your value – instead you choose a career that reflects your values.

When your career determines your value, it becomes very easy to overwork and overextend yourself, because your sense of identity is tied to performance. People who live like this often experience burnout, career insecurity, work anxiety and workplace competition, because the source of their confidence is not internal, and instead comes from workplace metrics or career honours. When they are not 'achieving' they feel worthless, and they are constantly chasing their next career high – rarely taking the time out to reflect on their achievements.

Instead, to feel of value, they must always be working towards something. I've been there before, and this is a dangerous cycle to be in, because you are in a race you can never win. There will always be 'more' to do and there will always be someone achieving 'more'. You will never be satisfied unless you are able to find identity outside your workplace achievements. And that's not to suggest your ambition will die when you do so. You can still be ambitious while separating your sense of self from your career results. How? Like Oprah said, when you centre intent and your values, the ambitions you have are driven, not by accolades, but by achieving something purposeful. Liking who you are helps you gauge what truly feeds you and not simply what looks impressive on paper. Your ambition is driven by how you can help others or something that makes you feel alive and nourished – instead of something that makes you appear successful to strangers or loved ones.

Liking who you are also determines what you will and will not tolerate in the workplace. Whether it's a toxic working environment, working for a company that goes against your beliefs or being in a draining job, you're able to recognise you deserve better and you prioritise choosing something different. Now that's not to say it's always easy – I understand that some people are dependent on their jobs more than others, based on a variety of responsibilities they may have, like a mortgage or children. Leaving a job the moment you feel discomfort isn't always doable, but even when it's not easy, being able to recognise misalignment and problems in your chosen job is valuable. And while you may not be able to shift roles or your career immediately, that awareness will support you with creating an eventual exit plan for the future.

Needs, Wants and Now

This activity is a great prompt for reflecting on your current job and the kind of job you want.

1. Grab a piece of paper and create three columns, titled 'Needs', 'Wants' and 'Now'.
2. In column one, I want you to list things you feel you need from a job role, like safety, stability, a steady income and respect. These things should be your job non-negotiables.
3. Next, you're going to list things you want from a job. For some of you it might be the freedom to work remotely, for others it might be working in a specific city. Maybe it's a job that enables you to work with your hands or leverage a degree you have? Think of everything you want from your job and write it down.
4. In the third column you're going to list all the qualities you see in the job you have now. Does your current job reflect all your needs? Does it meet a decent number of your wants? Or are your non-negotiables currently being negotiated? If the latter is true, reflect on which current work conditions go against these non-negotiables.

The point of this exercise is to help you understand your work requirements. Listing your needs and wants will help you to see the difference between comfort and core values. Maybe you'll come to discover that what matters most to you isn't a very high salary but having time for family. Or maybe you'd trade a fancy title for a job that makes you feel at peace and respected. Or maybe a certain amount of money *is* the motivator? The more you clarify what truly matters, the easier it becomes to make aligned decisions – whether that means staying where you are and setting new boundaries, or finding a new job that is better suited to you. When you list your needs, you remove the guesswork, and you stop chasing jobs that look good and instead you build a career that feels good.

Closing Thoughts

Finding work that reflects your values isn't about finding 'the dream job' in the eyes of strangers, your friends or even your family. It's about finding a job that is aligned with who you are. In a soft job, you like what you do and you like how you do it. And while, in times of survival, you may accept a job that meets a temporary need (like providing you with income or a sense of stability), long term, choosing softly means being in a career that reflects your values, your priorities and your intentions.

Your work shouldn't define who you are; it *should* reflect how you choose to live.

Self-reflection prompts

When you think about your current or most recent job, which parts of it feel most like you?

Do you feel proud when you describe your job or are you just thankful it pays the bills?

How does your current job align with your values?

How do you currently define career success?

What boundaries would you create in your current job to make your work feel softer or more sustainable?

If you could design a work day that truly reflects who you are, what would it look and feel like?

When you imagine your ideal workplace, what principles does it abide by?

What does being valued and respected at work mean to you personally?

Soft Courage: Protect Your Peace in a Hard World

It would be easy to end this book with a fairytale – one where softness exists everywhere, where peace is permanent and where choosing ease is always a viable option. But sadly, this isn't the world we live in and for many of us, existing in a society riddled with unfairness and 'isms', comes with challenges and hurdles that might make the journey to soft living tougher. While living softly shouldn't be mistaken for privilege, personal privileges often determine how easy it is to access a life of softness.

Whether it's gender, race, economic status or ableism, the world was built to be softer for some people. Furthermore, it's significantly easier to speak up for yourself when you're in a position of power, make healthy choices when you're financially comfortable, choose a fulfilling job when you come from generational wealth, set boundaries when your safety isn't threatened, or prioritise wellness when you have endless free time. Living a soft life looks different when you're navigating systems that make survival harder, and in all my writing about soft living, I can't ignore the elephant in the room...

Racism

Let's look at race from the perspective of womanhood. Racism and white supremacy have contributed to white women being heralded as the epitome of femininity throughout history, and in modern mainstream media.

'Purity', 'vulnerability' and 'helplessness' are qualities often associated with white women, while Black and Brown women are viewed as more masculine – often tied to adjectives like 'strong', 'aggressive' and 'resilient'. Just review archetypes like the 'girl next door' or 'damsel in distress' – both of which have been historically associated with white women. These archetypes have provided white women with the freedom to express a desire for support and assistance when needed. Their voices and their needs are often heard more loudly than those of their non-white counterparts, and subsequently their desire to live softly is approached with more understanding and care. Even as children, white girls are afforded more comfort and protection than little Black girls. In fact, I remember experiencing this as a young child myself.

When I was in primary school, I was relentlessly bullied. Despite my bully and I both being seven years old, she was much taller and bigger than I was, and she was white. I had reported the bullying to various teachers at the time, and nothing seemed to change. I also reported it to my mother who further escalated it with my teachers, but had no luck.

Eventually, my mother was fed up and gave me some rather controversial advice. 'Just beat her up,' she said. My mum was convinced that the girl was bullying me because she believed I'd never stand up for myself but that once I did, she'd leave me alone. So, one summer afternoon, I summoned up the courage to defend myself.

The girl came over to pick on me after she caught me crying following being hit in the stomach by a football the boys were kicking. The second she opened her mouth, I went for her – slapping and pulling as best as I could for seven years old. Eventually, teachers pulled us off each other, and while I don't condone violence as an adult, it worked. I was surprised at how instantly the constant torment at school ceased – but I was also surprised at how quickly I was painted as the villain.

On the day it happened, I remember seeing all her friends hugging her. I remember her crying and all the teachers consoling her. I remember being harshly scolded for hitting her, despite the fact she had been bullying me the entire year and had hit me before. As a child I was so confused. 'Why is everyone upset with me now, when nobody was upset with her when she was being so awful to me?' That was my first experience of not feeling seen or believed, and I quickly realised that as a young Black girl, I wasn't functioning in a world that offered me the same level of grace.

When a white women cries, she is often comforted and believed, while Black and Brown women may hesitate to shed tears, should they be questioned.

I've witnessed how from childhood through to my teens and adulthood, Black and Brown women simply aren't given the patience and understanding that white women are awarded. Just look at something as common, natural and life-threatening as giving birth.

In 2023 the US Centers for Disease Control and Prevention (CDC) shared data confirming that Black women have a maternal death rate more than three times higher than white women. Similarly, in the UK, an investigation led by Oxford Population Health's National Perinatal Epidemiology Unit, found that from 2020–22 Black women remained three times more likely to die during childbirth compared to white women. Socio-economic factors certainly play a part in this statistic but underpinning everything is racism. A UK parliamentary report published by the Health and Social Care Committee in 2025 found that 'Black women in England continue to face disproportionately poor outcomes in maternity care.' The report, titled 'Black Maternal Health', stated: 'We heard of a culture where women, particularly Black women, are not listened to and their concerns are not taken seriously. This is reinforced by bias and stereotyping underpinned, in some cases, by racist assumptions.' This disparity in maternal mortality clearly highlights how racial privilege influences whether a woman is listened to and believed. Simply put, not being white is costing some women their lives.

Black and Brown women live in a world that has made us hyper-vigilant. Racism in the form of stereotypes, microaggressions or direct abuse makes it harder for us to rest mentally and emotionally. When you navigate the world as a non-white woman, you are chronically alert and this alertness can often leave little room for softness, as we have been taught to perform strength with the awareness that the world will not extend grace to us in the same way. While white women are entitled to softness, Black and Brown women often feel as if we must earn it. Coupled with this, white supremacy has provided white women with easier access to rest and ease. Both of which require safety and security – two things that are awarded to them more than women of colour.

So How Do You Live Softly When You're Black and Brown?

You are still entitled to your choices, and for that reason, you must always choose what you feel is best for you. Where the world may not advocate for you, advocate for yourself, and when people try to silence your voice, speak loudly. But in all your choosing and self-advocating, remember that you do not need to perform strength every day.

> You're allowed to display vulnerability, you're allowed to rest without guilt, to love without fear, and to express yourself without apologising. Living softly doesn't mean you must ignore challenges, but don't let the challenges you face talk you out of approaching life with gentleness and ease.

Being Black or Brown and soft is not weakness, and your identity shouldn't be defined by your ability to endure, nor does your value need to be proven through suffering. You deserve care, love and rest. And in a world that doesn't offer it to you naturally – take it for yourself.

Economic Pressure

Just as race shapes how easily we can access softness, so does class, because privilege doesn't just come down to racial identity – it's also connected to economic stability. When money is scarce, softness can feel like an unattainable luxury, because economic pressure is one of the most significant barriers to soft living.

The ability to live healthily, take a mental and physical break, access decent healthcare, find great work opportunities, and much more, is often tied to the money we have and the social networks we are connected to. It would be pretentious to behave as if a severe lack of funds doesn't keep people in a constant state of survival mode – because it does. When you're struggling to figure out how to keep your electricity on or where you'll find money for your next meal, living softly is the last of your concerns. You're not considering buying the healthiest food, or accessing wellness services, because all you want to do is survive, and thriving won't take up mental space until survival is no longer a daily priority.

If you're under financial pressure, you must define soft living in a way that works for you – focusing on the things you *can* control. Softness begins with how you speak to yourself when life feels hard. Talk to yourself with the same tenderness you'd give to someone you love, and don't beat yourself up for being under financial constraints. Also remember that even if your environment feels chaotic, you can create small rituals of softness – like taking a walk, journalling, spending time with people who bring you joy, meditating, listening to music that makes you feel at peace, and more.

When I was in my twenties, I was living on an overdraft – pay cheque to pay cheque, but I still found time for moments of peace which reminded me that my body still deserved gentleness. Allow soft living to influence how you show up for yourself, and also, how you connect with others – via your soft community, your willingness to be open and vulnerable, or create moments for closeness in romantic relationships. I want you to remind yourself that softness can also exist beyond things that require payment. In fact, some of the most powerful forms of soft living are priceless.

Sexism

As a woman living in a patriarchal society, it's easy to believe that our value must be proven, and rest can only be granted to us after we have met everyone else's needs. Women have long been told that our worth is tied to our productivity – particularly when it comes to household labour, as well as our willingness to be pleasant and accommodating. In fact, endless studies show that women take on most of the unpaid labour – from domestic work to caregiving – at a time when women are also working to bring home income, when many of us are navigating life constantly on the go, at the beck and call of someone else's needs, and are exhausted. The expectation has long been that as women we must put ourselves last, and everyone else first.

Economic inequality further makes life challenging for us. Whether it's the gender pay gap or glass ceilings – the truth is, living softly can feel like they're harder to overcome when you're a woman. We know that financial security is another form of freedom, but without access to equal pay, it's easy to question whether we will ever feel as free as men do. Even when we work as hard as men or better, our assertiveness and intelligence is sometimes looked down on and labelled unfairly.

The same way racism shows up in healthcare, sexism does too. Women's health is often treated like an afterthought, with not enough consideration in research. And when we are considered, our bodies are politicised, and our autonomy taken away. Just assess how a country as 'forward thinking' as the United States rolled back the right for women to access abortion services.

On 24 June 2022, the US Supreme Court overturned the constitutional right to abortion nationwide – ending protections that had been in place for nearly fifty years. The change meant each state could determine its own abortion laws. As I type, it is 2025, and almost half of US states have banned or limited access to abortion, and more are moving towards tighter restrictions. The impact of this constitutional change has impacted the lives of many women and families, including the family of Nevaeh Crain.

In 2023, eighteen-year-old Nevaeh Crain died following medical delays while experiencing a miscarriage under Texas' broad abortion ban. Nevaeh visited three different hospital emergency departments within a 24-hour period, before eventually passing away. Despite showing signs of sepsis, she was sent home because her foetus still had a heartbeat. In a state like Texas, which threatens prison time for interventions that end a foetal heartbeat, doctors are hesitant about intervening in miscarriages or other pregnancy related complications. In a statement from Brittany Fonteno, President & CEO of the United States National Abortion Federation, 'Nevaeh died because emergency room doctors in three separate hospitals feared legal retribution from anti-abortion extremists and lost precious hours debating how to treat Nevaeh. Candi Miller, Amber Thurman, Josseli Barnica, and now, Nevaeh Crain. These are just some of the first people we know of who have lost their lives because of extreme and dangerous abortion bans that denied them essential, emergency care.'

If you want to live softly in a world shaped by misogyny and sexism, then you mustn't ignore injustice. It's very easy to behave as if injustice doesn't exist to 'protect your peace', but silence only enables the systems working against you to further work against you – making your life harder in the long run.

Earlier in this book I mentioned that an important part of living softly is accepting being disliked, and this is a fine example of how being disliked can be purposeful. Like Brittany Fonteno, sometimes you will have to raise your voice and hold people accountable in a way that makes them uncomfortable, and sometimes you will need to demand equity to make *your* life more comfortable.

Ableism

Living softly is harder when you're disabled or managing a chronic illness, because the world isn't designed around your needs. Things other people take for granted, like earning money, making friends, keeping plans, or simply showing up, can require careful planning, extra recovery time, or even additional resources. Soft living asks us to slow down, to listen to ourselves, and to build fulfilment from the inside out, but when the world wasn't designed with disabled or chronically ill people in mind, it can make soft living feel complicated. With that said, complicated doesn't mean impossible. It simply means that softness must be approached with strategy.

For example, if you have a disability or chronic illness, things like building your soft community may feel tougher. When it's easy to show up, socialising certainly feels more straightforward, but living with a disability and chronic illness often makes showing up unpredictable. Whether it's mobility challenges, pain flares, fatigue or more, these things can shrink your social circle because not everyone understands what you're going through. But the point is, people who can't hold space for your humanity were never soft places to land anyway. For disabled and chronically ill people, friendship works best when you explain your boundaries early (without apology), when you prioritise your energy and wellbeing (for example, through online catch-ups or shorter visits), and when you connect with honesty and transparency. And the same is true for finding love. Soft love for you is built on understanding, patience, compassion and a willingness to learn. You deserve a partner who doesn't define you by your condition, while also respecting your differences. Like everyone, you deserve a partner who values you.

> Going where you're valued is an important aspect of living softly, but for anyone with a disability or chronic health condition, it's even more vital.

Even in the context of your career, finding employers who value people over output will make such a difference to your working life. In addition, choosing roles with flexible hours or remote options will give you the freedom to safeguard your wellbeing, while also feeling like your career trajectory isn't being impacted. And it's important that you honour your capacity in the process. As much as rest is essential for everyone, it's even more important for people who have a chronic illness. But as I shared earlier on in this book, people judge rest when it doesn't look earned, and it's not uncommon for people with disabilities or chronic illness to be mislabelled as lazy. But your rest is not up for debate. Set boundaries around your energy and give yourself permission to prioritise recovery without guilt. Soft living is not about proving anything. It's about doing what is best for you.

Living softly with disability or chronic illness isn't about escaping challenges. It's about meeting the challenges you face with courage and compassion. It's about designing a life where your body isn't the enemy, and your needs are not inconveniences. The world may not have been built for you, but your soft life can be.

Closing Thoughts

The world isn't soft for everyone – not when racism, sexism, classism and ableism still shape who gets ease, abundance and gentleness. Some of us must face challenges that others can't even fathom. But even in a world that can feel unfair, your life doesn't have to mirror that harshness. You can still control the controllables. You can still create softness by choosing relationships that pour into you, finding work that honours you, and crafting a life that fulfils you.

I'm also not going to pretend there won't be seasons when softness isn't possible, and survival comes first. These will be the moments when you're navigating a crisis or simply doing whatever you can to make it through the day. But soft living isn't about performing or living under pretence. You can acknowledge the hard times, yet still find ways to return to softness when life gives you room to breathe again.

In living softly, I don't want you to deny that hardship exists, but I do think you should refuse to let your hardships harden or define you, because softness isn't about living in a soft world. It's about finding joy and satisfaction living in a world that can sometimes be hard.

Self-reflection prompts

Do you benefit from any privileges that make living softly easier for you?

Do you experience any challenges that make living softly harder for you?

When was the last time you felt safe enough to fully rest?

How have you been rewarded for being strong, and how has that made it harder to be soft?

Who or what helps you return to softness when the world feels heavy?

What aspect of your life hardens you the most?

Soft Future: Embrace Change During Times of Uncertainty

The world is changing faster than we can fully process. In fact, in my thirty-six years of living, the changes have never felt quite so rapid. There was a time when the journey through life appeared relatively set in stone – you'd pay attention in school, get good grades, enter higher education, graduate, get a job, work your way up the ladder, find a partner, marry, buy a house, have children, work a little longer until you retire and then finally, enjoy the fruits of your labour.

The world no longer looks so 'traditional' now. Accessing higher education is no longer a prerequisite for getting a high-paying job, living to work for many people is less appealing than working to live, marriage rates have declined as marriage is no longer viewed as a necessity, owning a home often feels unattainable with rising house costs across the globe, fewer people are having children or even desire them, and the age of retirement isn't so fixed. The life our parents and grandparents lived looks considerably different from how we live, and every day things change more and more.

One very noticeable change I'm personally witnessing is in the development of new technology – particularly artificial intelligence. AI has changed the landscape of many industries, from corporate to creative, and tools have been formed that can plan, design, compose, communicate and so much more. In many ways, algorithms work faster than human minds can, leaving many of us questioning where we will even fit in. From AI musicians to AI assistants, models, marketers, artists and even recruiters, the work landscape can feel very uncertain, no matter where you are in your career. And while these technological advancements can make some parts of life feel easier, they can make the future feel unstable.

As much as I love what I do, I'd be lying to you if I said it was impossible for AI to recreate my work and I have no doubt that AI could write a book in super quick time. It may not be as personal or as emotive, but the truth is a single AI model has access to a wider range of information than the human brain can fully recall, and many people are rightly nervous about it.

That feeling of nervousness and instability can also be felt in how we relate to our environment. What we once assumed was constant – the weather, the seasons and the air we breathe, is now a cause for concern. Environmental issues are part of everyday discussion, and the future feels more vulnerable for many of us. This environmental uncertainty impacts plenty of our decisions – including the car we choose to drive, the way we shop, and whether we even want to have children. And as concerning as climate change is, it reminds us how precious our environment is and emphasises the importance of adaptation.

So much of what we thought was fixed, really isn't so certain any more – yet during such uncertainty, one thing that remains is our capacity as individuals to choose how we negotiate this world. In a world that is constantly evolving and reinventing itself, we can choose to do the same. Being open to change is at the heart of living softly.

Change is inevitable – change of our friendships, our bodies, our jobs, our relationships or our environment... It pays to embrace change, whether it's seasonal or a sudden shift, because when you resist it, life becomes an unending battle to try and keep things as they were. Even when it comes to things like AI, as frightening as it may appear at first, at some point we must accept that it isn't going away.

When the internet was introduced, some people were fearful, but the people who chose to adapt, learn and shift inevitably flourished through that period of change. Jobs were created, an element of ease was introduced to the working world, and people got more creative. Did it come with some negatives? Of course. As an example, the birth of the worldwide web gave criminals a reach they never had before – but it also brought a lot of good too, and the people who were able to spot the silver lining often benefitted from it.

This is exactly what is happening with AI. I'm seeing people make money from the introduction of AI platforms – either because AI has made their work easier or unlocked resources and ideas for them, or because the introduction of AI has opened up a new range of high paying technical jobs. Even in my own life, I use AI as an unblocker – to answer questions I'm confused about or to help me generate ideas when my own brain feels stuck. I could have let my nervousness about this new technology paralyse me into rejecting it entirely, but instead, I choose to evolve with the times.

Allowing yourself to relax into change and adapt, eases the mind, and helps you to see change and/or endings not as failures but instead as new beginnings. Being open to change also allows for your growth as it encourages you to be open to learning and prevents you from being tied to old ways of working, an old version of yourself, outdated tools, or even personal opinions and habits that you have outgrown.

> When you're open to embracing the future despite what it may bring, you begin to trust that softness can exist even in times of uncertainty. You accept that there are certain things you cannot control – and thus, worrying over them is futile.

But how do you remain full of optimism when you're inundated with news and updates from every direction? There always seems to be something new going on, and for the most part the reporting rarely seems positive. We are constantly overloaded with negative and stress-inducing information – whether that's online or via television, and it can get overwhelming.

In the same way I recommend being open to change, I also recommend administering boundaries when necessary. Being intentional about the information you consume, when you consume it and why you consume it, helps to reduce your anxiety about the state of the world, and by extension, your future. But note, I'm *not* saying you should embrace being uninformed.

Being 'intentional' about the news and information you consume is not the same as consuming nothing. It's still important to have a good understanding of current affairs so you're not operating with ignorance. You just need to curate your information and news intake so you can remain aware without feeling overwhelmed. Asking yourself why, when and how you consume news is at the crux of your curation process. Why do you want to be in the know? Do you want to be informed so you can make better decisions? Do you want to be able to hold your own during conversations? Do you want to feel like a responsible citizen? Or are you consuming for consumption's sake – as a form of escapism or boredom? If there is a good reason for your desire to consume, then you need to map out the *when*? Do you need live updates and broadcast notifications constantly active on your phone? Do you need news constantly playing in the background while you work? Or can you set aside time for your intake of news?

Keeping up to date doesn't even have to be a daily thing – it's OK to schedule a weekly round-up. I don't even watch the news every day. I take in what I can, when I feel comfortable. I'm also selective about where I get my content – which is the *how*. There are certain outlets I will never refer to because I find them misinformed and full of bigotry, while there are other outlets that I feel approach current affairs with more range, nuance, fairness and perspective. No mainstream news outlet will ever be 100 per cent neutral as they all have their own motives and agendas – but that's not to say some are undeniably more informed than others. You can also diversify what you count as 'news'. I'm personally not always watching TV. Sometimes I listen to podcasts, check YouTube, or follow social media updates from qualified individuals I trust, who also share news with solutions in mind, and hope.

Mixing in culture, art, sport and science also helps to broaden my world view without making me feel so overwhelmed. And in and amongst any chaos I may hear/read about, or anything that sits outside my control, I choose to focus on what I *can* control.

Focusing on what you can control is one of the simplest ways to live a gentle life of peace – especially when thinking about the future. Obsessing over the uncontrollable leaves you anxious with no real opportunity to administer any change – whether it's worrying about what's ahead, how AI is taking over, climate change, people's opinions, or the economy... Unless you can do something to change it, worrying about it just drains you of energy.

Shifting your energy towards your own choices, thoughts, attitude, routines and boundaries is one way to reclaim your power in the face of uncertainty, because to put things frankly, finding peace in life isn't simply tied to an absence of problems – it's largely about perspective too. Do you allow problems to consume and control you?

Now in saying this, I'm not suggesting that in the preservation of your peace you should stop caring about anyone outside your immediate network, or that you should never seek out opportunities to help others and perhaps even influence a situation that feels outside of your control. For example, just because you cannot influence the outcome of a war as an individual, doesn't mean that you shouldn't donate to charities supporting refugees, or that you shouldn't protest for a ceasefire.

In both those examples, you can be responsible for *your* choices, not the choices of a majority – or the world for that matter. In being responsible for yourself, you can still do your part but without the burden of feeling responsible for outcomes that were out of your control. So, when you do block out time to listen to the news and you hear something that makes you anxious or afraid, you can choose to limit your consumption so as not to feel helpless (because after all, global issues can feel paralysing), or if you have a desire to help, you can consider what's actually within reach for you, like donating, volunteering or even voting.

To add, being anxious about things you can't control consumes so much passive energy. Instead, turn that anxiety into compassion. What small thing can you do to turn your concern into contribution? And if you decide to help, do what you can within your limits. Empathy without boundaries can become very draining. In building your soft life, you need to learn to help others while also taking care of your wellbeing and soothing your nervous system. And while witnessing suffering is never nice, you should try not to let any negative moods totally consume you. There is no way you can be of true service to yourself or others when you are constantly on the brink of emotionally falling apart. At times you will need to take a step back and be gentle with yourself. Living softly in this context isn't about detachment, it's about regulated engagement.

Optimism is a Must

My friends and family regard me as quite an optimistic person. Even in the face of adversity, I can find something to be grateful for and look forward to. My mother is a very optimistic and hopeful woman, who possesses an abundance of faith. My optimistic abundance mindset came from her, and I believe it has helped me significantly in life – particularly when it comes to my outcomes.

My personal experience aside, numerous studies have shown that possessing an optimistic perspective is linked to better outcomes in life for health, wellbeing, longevity and more. One observational study set out to assess whether higher levels of optimism are associated with a longer life span. The 2019 study by Lewina O. Lee and colleagues, tracked about 70,000 women for ten years, and approximately 1,400 men for thirty years, and each participant engaged in surveys to determine how optimistic they were. The study, titled 'Optimism is associated with exceptional longevity in 2 epidemiologic cohorts of men and women', found that 'optimism is specifically related to 11 to 15 per cent longer life span, on average, and to greater odds of achieving "exceptional longevity", that is, living to the age of 85 or beyond.'

To put it simply, the study suggests that a positive outlook could help you live longer, and the researchers believed this may be because optimistic people recover faster from setbacks, handle stress better, and generally build stronger relationships. Further studies suggest optimism improves health outcomes in general, and one meta-analysis found this to be likely. The meta-analysis, published in the *Journal of the American Medical Association*, included 229,391 individuals from 15 studies, with follow-up periods averaging 13.8 years. The review, titled 'Association of Optimism with Cardiovascular Events and All-Cause Mortality', found that people with higher optimism levels had about a 35 per cent lower risk of having a cardiovascular event compared to less optimistic people. The review also suggests that higher optimism was associated with about a 14 per cent lower risk of dying from any cause, and the benefit of being optimistic seemed to apply across sexes, age groups and countries (although most data was from the US and Europe).

When research consistently finds that optimistic people live longer and have lower rates of disease, it proves that our mindset has real and measurable effects on the body. It's not just about being jolly, it's about how our beliefs influence our life. Maintaining an abundant, gentle and soft outlook can be just as important as our decisions – even in the face of challenges, change or uncertainty. And if science can prove that a hopeful mindset can lengthen our life, imagine what can happen when we start visualising the life we actually want, instead of simply reacting to the life we currently have.

A Soft Life Vision Board

If optimism is the belief that things can improve or work out, a vision board is the physical evidence that we believe it to be true. It's one way of saying 'this is what I'm working towards'. For those who are unfamiliar with what a vision board is, it is a visual montage of the life you want to live. It can be physical or digital – but the goal is to collect images, text, and sometimes videos that reflect the life you want for yourself.

I have a digital vision board that I regularly refer to, and it truly helps to keep me positive, hopeful and motivated. On it, I have a close-up photograph of an elderly married couple holding one another's hands, a modern mansion, the silhouette of three children, a photo of Bora Bora, the words 'New York Times Bestseller', a Bible verse, and much more. Arranging these things onto my own board acts as a reminder of my goals, which helps me to reach them – and there's science to back this up.

A 2024 study by Julian Voigt, Marius Jais and Hugo M. Kehr assessed how having a vivid vision of the future (rather than just a vague goal) helped people actually make progress towards what they want. The study, titled 'An image of what I want to achieve: How visions motivate goal pursuit', found that when people vividly imagine the future they want (not just listing goals, but actually picturing what it looks and feels like), they're more likely to make progress towards it. The study suggested that seeing your goals in your mind creates excitement and positive emotion, which makes you more motivated and committed to taking real steps. In other words, the clearer and more emotionally charged your vision is, the more likely you are to follow through.

When you gather visuals that resonate with you, identify not just the image, but the feelings behind them. When you look at a picture of your dream home, which feeling does it evoke? Peace, stability, freedom, love? How do you think you will feel when you are living there? Imagine that you are there right now – is your mind and body responding to that? Creating a vision board isn't about making a 'to-do list', it's about tuning into energy. It's a visual reminder of the version of yourself you want to nurture, not the one you're trying to prove to others. What do you want next year to bring? What about next month? Choose photos, words and imagery that capture how you want your life to feel, not just how you want it to look on the surface.

Closing Thoughts

The future will always be unpredictable and it's full of things we can't completely control, but uncertainty doesn't have to equal fear. When you choose to adapt and be flexible in the face of change or uncertainty, you can find opportunity, and remaining optimistic can help you create softness in a future that may seem hard. Having a clear sense of what you want your future to look like, will help you remain positive and focused – and while the journey may not always unfold exactly as imagined, that's part of the beauty of life. When we don't know what's ahead, we can imagine the positive possibilities.

In his play, *The Merry Wives of Windsor,* William Shakespeare wrote 'Why, then the world's mine oyster, / Which I with sword will open.' These words have evolved into 'the world is your oyster', with the Oxford Dictionary defining this idiom to mean 'you are in a position to take the opportunities that life has to offer'. You are most certainly in this position, and you know this, which is why you picked up this book. I know you want to change your life, and reading this book is just step number one. The rest is up to you. The world is your oyster, providing you believe this to be true.

Create your own vision board

Self-reflection prompts

What parts of the future feel uncertain to you right now, and which of those are within your control?

How do you usually respond to change, and how would you like to respond? What evidence from your past shows that you're capable of handling change, even when you didn't feel ready?

What helps you feel more optimistic and how can you build more of that into your days?

If you approached the next month with the assumption that good things are possible, what would you do differently?

What does your ideal future look like?

When you think about your ideal future, how does it make you feel?

What's one step you can take today that aligns with the future you want, even if the bigger picture is still unfolding?

Epilogue: Stepping into Your Soft Life

As you reach the end of this book, I hope you have begun to see soft living for what it truly is... It's not an aesthetic, nor is it merely a trend. Living softly is a meaningful and intentional way of manoeuvring through the world.

A soft life begins with self-love, which in turn helps you better shape your life by building meaningful relationships, harnessing good health, embracing community, developing an abundance mindset, and prioritising work that reflects your values. A soft life is a life that honours your energy, your boundaries, and the person you are becoming.

In living softly, I want you to know that you are deserving, and everything you want in life is not out of reach. Be kind to yourself as you walk into this new chapter of your life and be clear and honest with yourself about the things you need to do to create this life.

Along the way, nurture the friendships that nourish you and find strength in your community, but do that with the understanding that not everyone is for you, and that's OK – because you aren't here to please everyone. People may dislike you for choosing better, but with the self-love you are cultivating, that shouldn't damage your self-esteem.

I also want to gently warn you that as you evolve, you may lose people along the way because some relationships simply won't align with the person you are becoming. Letting go of people can be painful. Especially if they've been in your life for a while. It can unsettle your identity and challenge your sense of belonging, but sometimes we must lose people to find ourselves.

Sometimes we must shed elements of our past to step into a happier and more satisfying future. As painful as it may be to accept, the relationships that fall away might just be the ones that keep you anchored to a version of you that you have outgrown. But this is a part of soft living – evolving, growing and surrounding yourself with people who welcome your new habits, instead of people who criticise them. What matters most is the intention you hold and the belief you cultivate within yourself.

On this journey, remember to spend with intention. Don't make money your master, but instead, master your money. And choose a job not purely based on income or title, but one that reflects who you are, where you are in your life, and what you value. Your career should be fulfilling but it also shouldn't define you. As you build a fulfilling career, also make time for rest. After all, body no be stone. Your health matters, so please do what you can to prioritise it. Make better choices with the understanding that you only have one body.

With this said, it would be presumptuous of me to suggest things will be easy from here. On your journey to building your soft life, you will face challenges because growth always comes with growing pains. You may start strong and then slip back into old patterns of overworking, tolerating too much, or neglecting yourself. You may have seasons where your boundaries or self-esteem feel fragile. That doesn't erase your progress though. It simply means you're human. And in being human, you will stumble sometimes, but to live softly you must also be compassionate with yourself and remind yourself that it's OK to gently return to your journey whenever you may wander off-path. You may also have to deal with people who behave as if you don't deserve the life you are building. Whether it's because of your race, gender, economic status or disability, don't let that deter you. As I mentioned at the start of this book, soft life isn't a life reserved for the few.

Every boundary you set, every choice you make and every moment of rest you allow, moves you closer to the life you deserve – one filled with gentleness, abundance and ease. So, as you close this book, carry this with you:

> You are more than capable and more than deserving of building a soft life that feels aligned with what you want and who you are.

You are allowed to change. You are allowed to choose ease. You are allowed to protect your peace without apology. Even when the journey feels uncertain, trust that each small act of gentleness is reshaping your world from the inside out. May this be the beginning of a life that doesn't just look good but feels soft. May this be the start of your soft life.

Acknowledgments

There are so many people who have helped bring Soft Life to fruition, and I'm deeply grateful to each of you.

First and foremost, my biggest thanks go to Mireille Harper at Bloomsbury. Thank you for approaching me with the initial idea for this book and for believing in it from the very beginning. Your encouragement, vision, and support were the fuel behind my fire. This book simply would not exist without you, and I'm so thankful that we took this journey together.

To my incredible team at Dopamine, thank you for keeping everything moving behind the scenes. You navigated the logistics, admin and deadlines with real care - especially during one of the busiest seasons of my life. I'm impressed that you kept me on top of things while I was so busy planning my wedding and travelling! Your support gave me the space to focus on writing, and I'm endlessly grateful to you all for keeping me organised.

To everyone at Bloomsbury, thank you for believing in Soft Life and for all the work you've poured into planning, promotion and marketing. I appreciate every contribution you've made.

A special thank you to Amberlee Green for creating such beautiful illustrations. Your artwork has brought my book to life in a special way, and I'm so grateful for your talent and creativity.

And finally, to every single person who has ever picked up one of my books... Thank you. Your support has made this career possible, and it has given me the opportunity to keep sharing words that matter to me. Soft Life exists because of you. Thank you for reading my work, for believing in my work, and for allowing me to continue this journey. I never take it for granted.

Toni x

A Note on the Author

Toni Tone is a Sunday Times Bestselling author, award-winning podcast host and content creator with a global following of over 1.3 million. She is best known for being the internet's big sister, dispensing her advice on everything from relationships to careers, friendships, and life lessons.

January 2025 saw Toni launch her first solo podcast, *Toni Told Me*, which has quickly gained a loyal audience and earned her a nomination on the British Podcast Awards' 2025 shortlist for the Rising Star award. She has also hosted the BBC Sounds podcast *Money Moves*, and the Carolina Herrera podcast *Walk Tall*, for which her series won Bronze in the Business category at the British Podcast Awards.

Toni's debut book, *I Wish I Knew This Earlier: Lessons on Love* (2021), became an instant Sunday Times Bestseller, followed by *Take Note: Real Life Lessons* (2022), a powerful exploration of personal and professional growth. Her third book, *No F*cks Given*, was published in the UK in September 2025 and in the US in March 2026.

In 2024 she was shortlisted for bCreator's Lifestyle of the Year award, and she remains a longstanding Ambassador for the Young Women's Trust. She regularly delivers impactful campaigns for global brands including WhatsApp, PayPal, Max Factor and ITV

BLOOMSBURY TONIC

Tonic
/ˈtɒn.ɪk/
noun

A restorative for mind, body and spirit.
A spark that lifts, energises and inspires.
Something that leaves you feeling better than before.

At Bloomsbury Tonic, our books are created to nourish you. Each one is intended as a quiet pick-me-up, a steadying presence, and a reminder that feeling better doesn't have to be complicated.

Like any good tonic, these books are designed to invigorate and refresh. They offer new ways of seeing and living, while staying rooted in warmth, honesty and real life. You'll find ideas that are bold and thoughtful, but always human - grounded in experience, compassion and care.

Whether you're turning to this book for comfort, inspiration, practical guidance or a moment of calm, we hope it leaves you feeling restored - a little lighter, a little clearer, and gently energised for whatever comes next.